W9-ADW-943

EXPERIENCE, INFERENCE
AND GOD

LIBRARY OF PHILOSOPHY AND RELIGION

General Editor: John Hick, H. G. Wood Professor of Theology,
University of Birmingham

This new series of books will explore contemporary religious
understandings of man and the universe. The books will be
contributions to various aspects of the continuing dialogues between religion and philosophy, between scepticism and faith,
and between the different religions and ideologies. The authors
will represent a correspondingly wide range of viewpoints.
Some of the books in the series will be written for the general
educated public and others for a more specialised philosophical
or theological readership.

EXPERIENCE, INFERENCE AND GOD

John J. Shepherd

BOOKS
10 East 53d St. New York 10022
(a division of Harper & Row Publishers, Inc.)

© John J. Shepherd 1975

First published 1975 by
THE MACMILLAN PRESS LTD
London and Basingstoke

Published in the U.S.A. 1975 by
HARPER & ROW PUBLISHERS, INC.
BARNES & NOBLE IMPORT DIVISION
ISBN: 0–06–496235–0

Printed in Great Britain

i'm rhieni

a Judith

ac i'm Mamgu

er côf annwyl

Contents

Preface

This book is based on a doctoral thesis prepared in the Department of Religious Studies at the University of Lancaster under the supervision of Professor Ninian Smart and Dr James Richmond. I should like to express my gratitude to both for their continued help and encouragement.

There are three principal themes running through the study. One is concerned with the methodology of justification; one with the concept of God; and one with the assessment of actual theistic truth-claims.

Originally I envisaged carrying out a sort of mopping-up operation on such remnants of the rational defences of Christian belief in God as were left after the demolition job represented by works such as R. W. Hepburn's *Christianity and Paradox*, C. B. Martin's *Religious Belief*, A. Flew's *God and Philosophy*, and W. I. Matson's *The Existence of God*. Gradually, and initially mainly through the challenge of the relevant parts of H. P. Owen's *The Christian Knowledge of God* (which is perhaps surprising in view of the very different approach adopted here), I came to feel that the case for Christian theism was not after all hopeless. The result is the argument of the following pages, which thus represents a considerable change of view. The change will strike many readers as a lapse into error. It may well be so; but if so, then at least, I hope, interestingly or even fruitfully so.

1 Natural Theology and Religious Experience

Attitudes towards the question of the rational justification of Christian theism vary widely. The particular constructive approach developed here would doubtless benefit if preceded by detailed criticism of various alternatives, but reasons of space prevent this. It is worth broaching the argument, however, via the context to which it belongs.

I believe the veto placed on natural theology by Barthian and Wittgensteinian fideists can be shown to be incoherent; but apart from that, the present study may be interpreted as an attempted practical refutation of their positions. On the other hand, despite contemporary work on the ontological argument for example, the existence of God does not seem susceptible of conclusive proof – certainly not yet.

Between these two extremes lie various possibilities. Process thought would be a good basis for affirming God's existence – if only it furnished an acceptable interpretation of the cosmos; I hope to argue elsewhere that it does not. Other people urge that by the very act of striving to live we presuppose that life has a meaning in a way that can only be true if God exists as the ground of meaning; yet against this it may be insisted that even without God, men, whatever their ancestry or material composition or fate at death, are individuals of great value, no more to be rejected as worthless than a beautiful flower should be rejected as ugly simply because it will wither and die. Again, it is suggested that the acceptance of moral values presupposes a divine ground of moral value; yet if men are of great value simply by being men, it follows that they exert moral claims on each other, that they generate a network of moral obligations, and these in turn occasion the development of general or universal principles of conduct which are correctly graded as authoritative and as eliciting respect and obedience.

J. Macquarrie has urged the propriety of a new-style natural theology based on Heidegger's existentialism. A brief examination of certain of his views will provide a good entry into the main part of this study.

Firstly, he argues that if the existence of God functions as the conclusion of an inference or as an explanatory hypothesis, God is debased to an object, to a part of the world, thereby compromising his transcendence; secondly, that God must therefore be interpreted in terms of Being rather than *a* being; thirdly, that natural theology should uncover the roots of faith in Being in experiences of being itself; and fourthly, that the proper function of natural theology is to show that faith in Being is compatible with the facts of experience rather than to show that it is required by them.[1]

Theses one, two and four derive from the need to preserve divine transcendence. In response, let us observe first that much of the force attributed to the objection that God is being made part of the world derives from an ambiguity in 'world'. 'World' may be defined in a variety of ways, but two important senses are 'world' as 'the totality of what is', and 'world' as 'the spatio-temporal cosmos'. Now certainly, if inferential natural theology made God part of the cosmos it would be both religiously and philosophically inadequate; yet given that God is not nothing it cannot avoid making him part of the totality of what is. The crucial point then, however, is in what sense he 'is', or what interpretation is to be given to talk of his transcendence; and indeed, provided that his (religious) transcendence is safeguarded, it follows that from a theological (or presumably any other) standpoint it is immaterial whether he is in a way an object or whether his existence is a hypothesis – or of course whether he is *a* being, for clearly he will be anything but a 'being among beings'.

Now a proper analysis of transcendence will be developed later. Nevertheless, a foundation for such an analysis may be suggested in the light of which rejection of the very possibility of an inferential natural theology is revealed to be unwarranted.

It is instructive to take as the starting-point an objection to the notion of divine transcendence that has been raised by such philosophers as R. W. Hepburn and A. Flew. The theological view is that God is beyond the cosmos but is able to act on and in the cosmos. The objection is directed at this use of 'beyond', 'on' and 'in'. The essential meaning of these words derives from their application in an intra-cosmic context; they are being stretched to breaking-point when applied to the relations between the cosmos and a being allegedly 'other' than the cosmos or a part of the cosmos. 'We know well enough that the world [cosmos] is not a box with sides, a field with boundaries; yet when we speak of insides and outsides, withins and beyonds, we are forced to think of it in exactly that sort of way, as a kind of limited object. And when we realise that this has been happening, we may well have serious misgivings as to whether our words have had meaning.'[2] There is a story about a child who one Sunday at breakfast asked his father where God was. 'Everywhere', came the reply. After a pause in which he digested this the child pressed the further question, 'Is he in this room?' 'Yes, indeed', answered the father. Pause. 'Is he in this cup?' 'Well, yes, I suppose he is', came the reply, albeit somewhat hesitantly. 'Right, got him!' cried the child, triumphantly clamping his hand over the top of the cup. Now theologically the error is grievous; but philosophically can it be corrected?

The suggestion that it can arises from consideration of the fairly widely held view that to be a person is to be more than a collection of material organised in a particular way. According to this dualist thesis my body and brain are spatio-temporal, and there is no problem about saying that they are in the world; but there are problems about identifying myself with my body, for my mind, although temporal, is not spatial or at least not in the same way (or it is not straightforwardly in the same space) as my body – and I am more intimately related to my mind than to my body, if I am not indeed to be identified with my mind. Yet if I am not my body, and if only my body and other physical entities can be straightforwardly said to be in the world, in what sense can *I* be said to be in the world?

Now the interesting thing about such a case here is that although it is not infrequently said to be false, it is much less frequently declared to be meaningless. Yet if it is not meaningless, then there is no reason why theological talk about transcendence should be meaningless. In the case above we should certainly want to say that I *am* in the world; but strictly speaking we should have to say that I am 'in' the world, where the inverted commas indicate the mystery of relating non-spatial or non-physical 'I' to spatial, physical 'world'. Moreover the mystery seems irreducible. We have a derivative or analogical use of 'in' modelled on the straightforward empirical use, yet we cannot specify the meaning of the analogical 'in' in non-analogical terms. Its meaning is 'indispensably non-literal' rather than metaphorical.[3] Yet if the meaning of 'in' may be stretched in this way for purposes of talking about persons (or about 'selves' as it may be put), who is to say that talk about God acting 'in' the world involves stretching meaning to breaking-point? Moreover, why should one not say that God is 'beyond' the world? Such a use of 'beyond' is irreducibly analogical, but it now appears that this need not be considered a fatal weakness. The same point may be made with regard to God acting 'on' the world, or indeed, taking 'world' now to refer to the totality of what is rather than the spatio-temporal cosmos, with regard to God existing 'in' the world.

If then, as seems natural, we model God-talk on I-talk and conceive of God as the 'supreme Self', it appears possible to speak meaningfully of his transcendent existence in the sense indicated. But this sense embraces (or is able to embrace) the notion of God as an existent entity, *a* being. And it will be argued later that it can be developed, without disturbing the embrace, into a full, religiously satisfactory concept of transcendence. Even at this stage, however, the possibility of such development should be clear; as also indeed the possibility of its being combined with an inferential natural theology, for it would now appear to be as legitimate in principle to argue to the existence of God as to argue to the existence of other minds. This does not presuppose, incidentally, that other minds are known primarily by inference. The suggestion is that inferential justification is possible, or that the quest for inferential justification is not in principle misguided; and as with other minds so too with God, since both are (if they are at all) 'in' the world rather than in it.

If this line of thought is sound, then it holds irrespective of the truth or falsity of mind–brain dualism. It is the meaningfulness of the dualist thesis that is at stake here. Yet what if the meaningfulness of the thesis be denied? The short answer is that its meaningfulness may be reasserted by those to whom it seems intelligible unless the denial of meaningfulness follows from a theory of meaning which they accept. The general problem of intelligibility will be dealt with separately, however.

Yet does not the preceding argument err by proving too much, for does it not follow that I too am transcendent? It should be remembered, however, that non-spatial existence is only one strand in the concept of transcendence. And although there may be a sense in which I partially transcend the physical universe, this is entirely compatible with or indeed in positive harmony with (most) religious belief.

It seems plausible to suppose then, certainly provisionally, that the concept of divine transcendence is not necessarily incoherent; that it accommodates the notion of God as a being without degrading him to the status of the cosmos; and that it permits attempts to work out a sound inferential natural theology.

It should be added with regard to the notion of God as *a* being that it is entirely in line with traditional piety and thus with the living roots of theistic belief. This being so, and since it seems to be a necessary condition of the intelligibility of talk about God that it should at least imply that he is *a* being, whole-hearted adoption of the view that he is *a* being is infinitely preferable to unavoidably obscure (and thus confusing even where not baffling), at best dubious and at worst ridiculous attempts to articulate a theology dedicated to the conjunction of 'There is no divine, transcendent entity (quality, substance)' and 'Atheism is false' by the existentialist proposal that God is Being.

Thus, Macquarrie's first two theses are certainly questionable, and the fourth is consequently also weakened. Now the fourth thesis is indeed crucial. Its acceptance presupposes the inapplicability of Occam's razor to theistic belief; yet theism should not be exempt from this principle whose claims on a rational person's allegiance are overwhelming. Indeed, analysis reveals the principle to be rooted in the deepest level of rational thought. For it asserts that, particularly perhaps with regard to objects other than inescapable empirical ones, one should not believe that an entity exists without good reasons for the belief; and the giving of good reasons for such beliefs is an apparently universal practice, certainly embracing all the types of human society of which we have any knowledge. There is every justification therefore for regarding it as an independent criterion (independent, that is, of restrictive cultural conditioning) to be employed in the task of determining the world's contents ('world' meaning here 'the totality of what is'). Its universality may be seen as a sign of its necessity for man, and its reliability may be judged by its apparent success in practice.[4] Belief in God must, then, be subject to the principle of parsimony; and nothing less than inferential justification, showing not only that belief is compatible with the facts of experience, but also that it is actually positively called for by them, satisfies this criterion.

This conclusion might be disputed by an appeal to religious experience. Here Macquarrie's third thesis is relevant. Although natural theology is not to provide inferential justification, it is to furnish a foundation for theology, and this it does by elucidating certain inescapable experiences. His emphasis here connects with the emphasis, typical of many modern thinkers, on various forms of experience, broadly characterised as religious, as a basis for belief. Their concern derives partly from a fear that religion might be subordinated to cold, rationalistic metaphysics. Certainly, where possible, this should be avoided – the emphasis on religious experience is salutary; but can experience without inference provide a rational basis for belief? If not, however, may religious experience be retained as a basis for inferential justification, thus getting the benefits of both?

Several possibilities arise here. Let it be said first, however, that Macquarrie sees faith as rooted in experiences, not initially religious, of being itself. The meaning of this is obscure. Nor are its prospects for use in natural theology improved by subsequent moves to talk of the grace of being and the grace of Being. Briefly, Macquarrie's position is either unintelligible; or illegitimately one-sided in its emphasis on the benevolence of existence, compared for example with Buddhist pessimism; or covertly inferential in the move from experience to Being; or implicitly reliant on the self-authentication of experiences of the grace of being; or a mixture of these. Thus, unless the notion of self-authentication is both admissible and applicable, his position is unsatisfactory; but the self-authentication issue, of course, is also relevant, and frequently crucially so, to other appeals to religious experience.

Perhaps there is a place for self-authentication – for example in connection with memory. Some things I *know* simply by remembering. I now *know* that the above words have just been written by me – but no one saw me, and neither a handwriting expert nor a scientist could date the script to the nearest minute, so empirical verification seems ruled out. Yet even if the notion of self-authentication is admissible, is it applicable to religious experience? If it were, inferential justification would indeed be unnecessary despite Occam's razor; but since reports of religious experiences contradict each other about what is allegedly disclosed in them, any appeal to self-authentication is nullified. Perhaps some experiences are self-authenticating; but since sincere claims to self-authentication conflict (cf. experiences of the grace of Being versus pessimistic experiences), they should be regarded sceptically by all – even, where possible, by those to whom they seem to occur. Were there intersubjective agreement about the kinds of experience and/or their interpretation, the case would be different (cf. the importance of intersubjective agreement in empirical verification and falsification).

It is arguable that the case of mysticism is in fact different; that although intersubjective agreement about doctrinal interpretation is lacking, there is basic agreement among mystics that their experiences disclose a transcendent being or state. This is offset, however, by the fact that it seems possible to provide a naturalistic explanation of mystical experiences. The mystic trains himself in effect to suspend the application of basic concepts and categories such as 'time and place and number and quantity and multiplicity' (Meister Eckhart), and his claims concerning ineffability, loss of individuality, abrogation of the subject–object distinction, union with or absorption into the infinite and so on are therefore in a sense not surprising – are indeed almost predictable. Moreover, as Hepburn suggests, following up this line of argument, our normal sense of our powers and limits is fostered by a utilitarian or practical view of the world, and 'when that view is suppressed, there can come the sense of exhilarating expansion or liberation that is often described in the mystical literature'.[5] If a naturalistic explanation of mystical phenomena is available, however, then allegiance to Occam's razor should ensure that it is adopted; for it is then unnecessary to posit an extra entity or state such as God or Nirvana. Thus the basic principle of parsimony pre-empts the positive epistemological inference one might otherwise be tempted to draw from the unity of mystical experience.

The prospects, then, for any natural theology using religious experience alone seem bleak; and even for religious experience together with inference they are not rosy. Yet do the above remarks apply to all forms of religious experience? Is there no form which avoids both intersubjective disagreement and Occam's razor? I suggest that there is – the experience of contingency. This will be discussed at length shortly.

For the moment let me emphasise the magnitude of the general problem presented by Occam's razor. I have in effect urged in connection with moral experience, with the experience of life's meaningfulness, and to some extent with religious experience, that belief in God is not rationally warranted on those grounds since his existence is not required as an explanatory hypothesis. But can it ever be so required? It is arguable that it cannot.

Reference may be made here to T. R. Miles's paper 'On Excluding the Supernatural' in which he argues against dividing occurrences into those due to natural causes and those due to supernatural causes. His first move is to offer a 'stipulative' definition: 'I am stipulating that, whatever occurs, it shall not be classified as the work of a "supernatural" as opposed to a "natural" agency.'[6] Such a stipulation has an arbitrary air, but this is deceptive. It is not, Miles urges, an arbitrary personal choice but the reflection of a view or standpoint the consequences of rejecting which we may find unpalatable. On the other hand there can be no question of a logical demonstration of the necessity of the standpoint. What then is it, this standpoint? It is that of the genuine search for knowledge. Failure to adopt his stipulative definition, Miles argues, is incompatible with this. Why? It is accepted policy in scientific investigation to try to explain macroscopic events in terms of microscopic ones, in terms of the behaviour of molecules or genes and so on. 'Whatever we come across, therefore, if we are genuinely concerned to search for knowledge, we can never be satisfied with a classificatory principle which implies the possibility of saying "Further inquiry at the microscopic level forbidden".' More generally, the classification of any event as due to supernatural causes entails that all forms of natural explanation must be inappropriate and that the search for them, being necessarily fruitless, should be abandoned. 'My point is that *whatever* events we come across, and however much they surprise us, we should refuse to say this. In the interests of knowledge we have a duty never to stipulate in this way.'[7]

This justification of what may be called Miles's prescriptive methodological postulate of the search for knowledge, or more simply the principle of natural explanation, is taken here to be basically sound. Moreover, adherence to the principle of natural explanation has been vindicated magnificently in the growth of science. Yet theism now appears placed in a potentially acutely embarrassing situation. For on the one hand it has been urged that belief in God is not rationally justified unless he is positively called for by facts of experience – in effect, there must be facts which require him as their explanation. Now, however, on methodological grounds there apparently cannot be any such facts. I argue later that this is not the whole story; but it is an essential part of the introductory narrative, contributing to the framework of what follows.

It certainly appears, however, that no form of religious experience will be able to overcome the obstacle of Occam's razor without the aid of some form of inference, even if God does not feature in an explanatory hypothesis. Yet here too the difficulties are compounded, for the traditional forms of inference must be discounted. Deductive inference is ruled out, for it was in effect urged at the outset in connection with the ontological argument that a deductive proof from agreed premises, such that acceptance of the premises and denial of the conclusion is contradictory, is not available for theism. Syllogisms like: 'If finite being exists then infinite being exists; but finite being does exist therefore infinite being exists' are clearly question-begging, reaching the desired conclusion only if 'finite' includes as part of its meaning 'dependent on the infinite'. Inductive inference, on the other hand, must also be ruled out. Inductive inference may in fact be divided into two forms of inference. Firstly, there is the notion of inductive proof exemplified in the claim that whenever there is lightning it will be followed by thunder – a view of scientific proof which received the authority of J. S. Mill. Secondly, there is hypothetico-deductive proof, the current established view of the methodology of science since its decisive formulation by K. Popper.[8] The former involves a correlation between observed phenomena and thus cannot apply to God; use of the latter presupposes that empirical deductions can be drawn from 'God exists', thus allowing empirical verification or falsification to occur – a presupposition neatly rebutted by I. T. Ramsey.[9] Acceptance of the principle of natural explanation also counts against the relevance of hypothetico-deductive inference.

Yet to say that the existence of God is neither empirically verifiable nor empirically falsifiable in this manner is not to say that empirical fact neither counts for nor counts against the existence of God. Were that the case, then, granted the bankruptcy of the *a priori* deductive approach, there could be no evidence for his existence, and we should be obliged not to believe. Yet we should have to say too that objectors to Christian belief have been mistaken in urging the existence of evil and suffering as counter-evidence, and this is highly paradoxical. It is far more satisfactory to allow that empirical fact may count for and against the existence of God despite the impossibility of empirical verification or falsification in the scientific manner, and certainly this impossibility does not of necessity militate against the possibility of counting for and against.

The position so far may be summarised as follows. The rational justification required must take full account of Occam's razor, of the principle of natural explanation, of the need for inference, though neither deductive nor inductive as normally understood, and of religious experience. Let me now emphasise the last of these.

If religious experience, or some forms of it, could furnish a basis or figure importantly in a basis for inferential justification of theism, there could be a threefold advantage:

(1) In traditional natural theology there has always been a problem regarding the identification of the entity 'proved' with the God of religion (or indeed of the entity 'proved' by one argument with that 'proved' by another). If the argument is rooted

in religious experience there is a presumption at least that this gap will be overcome.

(2) If there is an intimate relation between the argument and religious experience there is a presumption that the argument will be drawing out implications of the experience, or depending on it in such a way as to avoid the charge sometimes levelled against natural theology, that it makes a mockery of religion through reaching conclusions by means other than those operative in common piety, thus reducing the latter to superstition:

> If the *valid* grounds for believing in God's existence [writes J. Baillie] are different from the grounds which have actually led the world to believe in it, then it is only by an accident of coincidence that there is anything in the world's faith at all . . . and the religious man finds himself in the doubtful position of a schoolboy who is fortunate enough to get the answer to his sum right, though his working out was wrong.

A similar point, but intended to qualify natural theology rather than undermine it, is made by A. Farrer:

> If belief has been reasonable, it has had a reason, and our only business must be to draw this out and re-state it. If we are the first to have found true reasons, we must condemn our predecessors in faith as simply superstitious. It would be as though Copernicus had been preceded by certain devout Sun-Worshippers, who had concluded that luminary to be the centre of our system because it is so useful and so beautiful. In that case his subsequent demonstration would hold a merely accidental relation to their previous opinion.[10]

(3) As J. Cook Wilson urges, 'a proof may seem correct and yet it does not quite satisfy us because it does not touch our feelings'.[11] There is a presumption that an argument rooted in religious experience will achieve a natural harmony between emotion and reason which eludes many a desiccated speculative metaphysical counterpart (which is not to say that it itself is not metaphysical).

The fulfilment of these three promises would be of outstanding importance.

Natural theology is traditionally intended, however, to be

efficacious for the outsider; and the outsider may well be someone in whose life religious experience has played but little part, and for whom therefore an argument rooted in such experience would not be significantly more existentially influential than any other. This is a real problem in connection with most forms of religious experience; yet there is one form of experience which is susceptible of either a religious or a nonreligious interpretation – the experience of contingency. Let me elucidate this by distinguishing as follows between two kinds of religious experience, henceforth referred to as religious experience$_1$ and religious experience$_2$:

(1) experiences which stand or fall epistemologically either (a) with their own religious interpretation or (b) with some other religious interpretation;

(2) experiences which do not so stand or fall.

Examples should make this clear.

(1) (a) A person has an experience which, correctly as far as the phenomenology of the experience is concerned, he describes as an encounter with the Virgin. There are two possibilities. Either he encountered the Virgin or he did not. If the former is the case then his experience 'stands' epistemologically with his interpretation of it; he thought it was the Virgin and it was. If the latter is the case, however, then his experience 'falls' with his interpretation of it, in the sense that he in fact encountered no one at all. It was not the case that he thought that he encountered the Virgin but in fact encountered someone else who said she was the Virgin (or so most of us would assume, though it is of course a logical possibility and one which visionaries may, for religious reasons, take to be a real possibility; this does not, however, affect the *meaning* of saying that an experience stands or falls with its own interpretation, and it will not prevent most people from taking visions to be a case in point). He was the subject of a vision void of cognitive value.

(1) (b) A Sufi mystic has an experience which he describes as union with Allah. Either the claim is true or it is not. If it is then it 'stands' as before. On the other hand if it is not, not because there is no God but because He is not Allah, He is let us say the Zoroastrian God Ahura Mazda, then *either* the mystic's experience 'falls' with his interpretation of it as in (a) – he did not in

fact experience union with anyone, it was an illusion; *or* it 'stands' with a different religious interpretation such as a sympathetically-minded Zoroastrian might provide, namely that he had union with (or perhaps intimate experience of) someone but not with whom he thought: because of his religious upbringing, training and so forth he thought that he was experiencing Allah whereas in fact it was Ahura Mazda. His experience in that case is not entirely void of cognitive value.

(2) The main candidates for experiences which do not stand or fall epistemologically in the way indicated are the sense of contingency and the sense of the numinous.

The theist's experience of contingency may roughly be described as the sense of the world and God in the cosmological relationship. This will be discussed at some length in the following chapters. For the moment suffice it to say that it involves a feeling of dependence on the deity.

This feeling will clearly not be shared by an atheist but he may well have an elusive sense of the precariousness of existence, or a sense of ontological shock at there being and continuing to be a world at all. Now these are important elements in the theist's experience too and both experiences may justly be called experiences of contingency. And while the atheist may dispute that the experience points to God, he need not dispute the fact that the theist's experience is valid up to a point. The theist is, he may say, misinterpreting it.

A similar claim has been made by Hepburn with regard to numinous experience. As used by R. Otto such experience is definitionally the experience of encountering deity. Hepburn has no belief in a deity and yet has had experiences so closely akin to those described by Otto that he feels they must be called 'numinous'. This non-theistic use of 'numinous' is, he feels, 'legitimately eccentric' because of the difficulties of accepting that there is a self-authenticating theistic reference in the experience. The theist may well be misinterpreting the experience.[12]

In reply to Hepburn, H. D. Lewis has argued that the theistic experience of the numinous differs in essential respects from any similar experience by a non-theist. There is no basic, neutral experience which may or may not be interpreted theistically.[13] This echoes an objection frequently lodged against the distinction between experience and interpretation with which we are operating, namely the objection that the interpretation is an integral part of the experience and cannot be skimmed off it. It may be agreed that there is a sense in which this is true, but it does not affect the distinction being made here.

Clearly, the theist's experience of the numinous *does* differ from the non-theist's; and it was urged above that the theist's experience of contingency differs from that of the non-theist. It does not follow from this, however, that there can be *no* sense in which one may speak of one kind of experience with two possible interpretations. It is no doubt a loose way of speaking but nevertheless useful and within limits valid. What is in fact being said is not that there is a neutral or a pure, uninterpreted core of experience which may be interpreted theistically or atheistically – for one or other of these interpretations (or perhaps an agnostic one composed of rapid alternations of the other two) is indeed part and parcel of the experience – but that if a theist became an atheist or vice versa he would recognise his 'new', 'different' experience of contingency or of the numinous as most intimately related to, or indeed a modified form of, his 'old' experience. To speak of it being 'the same' though differently interpreted would then be analogous to the way in which we speak of our growing, changing selves as 'the same'. Lewis's objection thus rests on a half-truth alone and does not dispose of Hepburn's contention. Moreover, as used here the distinction between experience and interpretation does not conflict with the generally accepted and surely sound view that *all* experience involves interpretation of some kind, for it does not involve any notion of an uninterpreted core.

There is a sense then in which experiences of contingency and of the numinous are susceptible of either a theistic or a non-theistic interpretation. Now in so far as this is true of numinous experience (and it is true provided we reject Otto's epistemology of the numinous), then a naturalistic account such as Hepburn's is to be preferred on the ground of Occam's razor. If numinous experience does not demand a theistic interpretation then we should not supply one. About numinous experience understood in this way nothing further will be said here. The case of the experience of contingency is more complex, however, and there are possible reasons for according it preferential treatment with regard to the law of parsimony, as we shall see.

Returning now to the intended efficacy of natural theology for the outsider, here is an experience which in its non-religious interpretation is surely available to anyone. If then an argument based upon it were to aim at persuading one to reinterpret the experience religiously, the condition of the existential efficacy of the argument would most often already be fulfilled, the experience being on the whole considered important by those who have it. As for those who do not, it may fairly be claimed that they are likely to be able to achieve it more easily, and to have fewer reservations about the value of trying to achieve it, than other forms of religious experience. (Though these issues naturally need to be considered in more detail.)

If the experience of contingency is promising in this respect, however, it is surely disheartening in another. For has not the argument from contingency been tried and tried again only to be found wanting? Yet that is good reason for avoiding the topic only if no new way of approaching it can be found, or if old objections cannot be circumvented or overcome. It may be, however, that they can. At any rate the possibility is sufficiently attractive, both methodologically and in respect of validity, to warrant exploration.

2 The Experience of Contingency

'Contingent' may be used in several different senses. It commonly refers to propositions, meaning that their truth may be denied without self-contradiction. This use will figure in later stages of the argument, but here 'contingent' is taken to refer to existents rather than propositions. The propriety of so doing has been denied by some, but since 'from actuality to possibility the inference is good' it suffices to provide objectors with a valid meaning of 'contingent' outside logic; and in fact they may be provided with at least five.[1] As a characteristic of existents contingency may mean: (i) dependence on God; (ii) dependence on other existents in the cosmos; (iii) transience; (iv) lack of ontological self-sufficiency; (v) capacity to arouse a sense of ontological shock. The last of these requires some explanation which will be provided in a moment, and in so far as the meaning of the fourth is less than transparent it should become clearer in due course. In any event it should be possible to see already that (iv) is more basic than (ii) or (iii) for it allows for the possibility of a temporally infinite substratum of energy as the basis of all existents in the cosmos, and unlike (i) it leaves the question of the existence of God open. On the other hand it does imply or indeed entail the notion of a cosmos-supporting-being which compensates for the ontological deficiency of the world with its own self-sufficiency (provided the notions of ontological self-sufficiency and lack of it be accepted provisionally in so far as they are immediately intelligible). Let us therefore begin with (v) which begs no questions at all. The issue to be decided may then be expressed as being in important part that of whether the experience of contingency in the fifth sense, or 'contingency$_5$', can be defended as a cognitive experience and on this basis identified with an experience of contingency in the fourth sense, or 'contingency$_4$'.

The experience of contingency$_5$ (henceforth referred to simply as 'the experience of contingency' unless that phrase is explicitly interpreted otherwise) may be said provisionally to find expression in the oft-quoted line from Wittgenstein's *Tractatus*, 'Not *how* the world is, is the mystical, but *that* it is'. And N. Malcolm has described how Wittgenstein once read a paper 'in which he said that he sometimes had a certain experience which could best be described by saying that "when I have it *I wonder at the existence of the world*. And I am then inclined to use such phrases as 'How extraordinary that anything should exist!' or 'How extraordinary that the world should exist!'"'[2] It is, we may say, an experience of ontological shock and wonder at there being and continuing to be a world at all. (Yet as we shall see, this is a provisional description only, because it is in fact ambiguous, concealing a difference between two rather different experiences. Thus in due course the experience of contingency$_5$ will need to be analysed into experiences of contingency$_5$ and contingency$_6$. As the distinction is of little or no importance yet, however, for now it is adequate to speak in more general terms of an experience of ontological shock.)

Characterised briefly thus, the experience appears able to offer satisfactory credentials of validity. It appears plausible to award it cognitive status on the grounds of intersubjective agreement. Thus it contrasts favourably with the types of experience discussed in the previous chapter. (*a*) It need be limited neither to adherents of a particular religion nor indeed of any religion; (*b*) when it occurs it appears to be more convincing than religious experience$_1$, in that a person ceasing to enjoy religious experience$_1$ as often as not continues to experience contingency, and indeed finds it difficult not to, long after religion has ceased to have any appeal; (*c*) although many people do not experience contingency, agreement among people who do is sufficiently impressive to warrant the conclusion that they are genuinely aware of something to which others, even if they are the majority, are blind. Therefore if there is any merit (and I assume that there is) in the epistemological views enshrined in scientific and everyday practice, according to which intersubjective agreement is crucial, it may be said that the experience of contingency is susceptible of verification and is indeed in part verified. Moreover it gives the impression that further verification is possible. To this extent therefore, unlike religious experience$_1$, we have no real cause to doubt it.

Much remains to be said, however, for the brief characterisation of the experience of contingency given above is deficient in an important respect (or does not describe the experience in its most developed form). The experience not only finds expression in exclamations like 'How extraordinary that anything should exist!', 'How extraordinary that the world should exist!', but also occasions corresponding questions such as 'Why is it that anything exists?', 'Why is it that the world exists?', 'Why is it that a world exists?', 'Why is there a world at all?' This means that if we do allow that the experience has cognitive status, what we commit ourselves to is the *propriety* of being *puzzled* by the fact of the world's existence, by its being and continuing to be. But problems arise concerning both (*a*) the nature of the puzzle and (*b*) any propriety that may be claimed for it.

(*a*) The questions which express the puzzle sometimes seem themselves as puzzling as the puzzlement from which they arise, as J. J. C. Smart points out. Of the question 'Why should anything exist at all?' he writes:

Logic seems to tell us that the only answer which is not absurd is to say, 'Why shouldn't it?' Nevertheless, though I know how any answer on the lines of the cosmological argument can be pulled to pieces by a correct logic, I still feel I want to go on asking the question. Indeed, though logic has taught me to look at such a question with the gravest suspicion, my mind often seems to reel under the immense significance it seems to have for me. That anything should exist at all does seem to me a matter for the deepest awe. But whether other people feel this sort of awe, and whether they or I ought to is another question. I think we ought to. If so, the question arises: If 'Why should anything exist at all?' cannot be interpreted after the manner of the cosmological argument, that is, as an absurd request for the nonsensical postulation of a logically necessary being, what sort of question is it? . . . All I can say is, that I do not yet know.[3]

Thus Smart pays impressive tribute to the importance of the question and of the experience of contingency, but remains largely agnostic regarding their import.

(*b*) Others are less kindly in their treatment; and here we encounter a positive refusal to allow any propriety to the puzzle whatsoever. Thus I. M. Crombie is taken to task by K. Nielsen for asserting that the sense of contingency gives rise to an 'intellectual dissatisfaction with the notion of this universe as a complete system'. What does this mean? asks Nielsen. Why 'intellectual', why not 'emotional'? It is our cultural practice, he continues, to seek explanations for occurrences *within* the universe, and in certain moods we may want to ask a question as to the explanation of the *totality* of things. But such a question is 'not a rational question'. 'It only strikes us, or strikes some of us in certain moods, as a rational, literal question because we have an emotional investment, resulting from powerful early conditioning, in so talking about the universe. We should not speak here . . . of an intellectual dissatisfaction, but of an emotional one born of our natural infant helplessness and our early indoctrination.'[4]

Two elements in Nielsen's criticism may usefully be distinguished. Puzzlement about the existence of the universe is (1) a culturally conditioned emotion, which (2) finds expression in improper questions.

Now it is no doubt true that Judeo-Christian conditioning has been influential, even crucially so, in provoking perplexity about the existence of the universe, but it does not follow that such perplexity when it occurs is *merely* or non-cognitively emotional. Indeed, reasons have been suggested above to the contrary. In particular, the experience of contingency often successfully outlives religious faith, or is enjoyed by adherents of no faith. Nielsen begs the question as to whether or not a mood may be a mode of awareness.

In order to substantiate this, however, it is necessary to take up Nielsen's second point and examine the *questions* which the mood precipitates. These are plainly not rational, he says. Why not? Certainly not *because* they arise only in certain moods, as is suggested in the passage quoted above, for that too would be question-begging, and doubly so. It would be to repeat the previous error and it would be to *assume* that the questions, once they had arisen, could under no circumstances be divorced from the emotion and treated purely intellectually as sound, rational questions. This indeed suggests a further difficulty with such a view, for it is arguable that the mood is as much a product of rational reflection as vice versa. This will indeed be urged later, and an attempt made to show that the questions are profoundly rational and that the experience of contingency has an important intellectual component. It is not a mere irrational mood.

But Nielsen continues: 'That there is no intellectual problem here, but an emotional harassment, felt as a philosophical problem, is evident enough when we reflect that we do not understand what we are asking for when we ask for a non-derivative, non-contingent, infinite being, by reference to which we might contrast ourselves as derivative, contingent or finite beings.'[5] Against this it will be argued that it *is* possible to indicate what we are asking for.

The preceding remarks suggest then that the strategy of the present argument needs to consist in important part in offering a basically single but three-sided defence of the experience of contingency as a mode of awareness or cognition – a defence which amounts to a justification of identifying contingency$_5$ with contingency$_4$. The three-sided defence is composed of (i) the argument from intersubjective agreement already outlined, based on that form or part of the experience which does not include world-contingency questions; (ii) a defence of the rationality of the questions arising out of or indeed forming part of the experience of contingency – questions which, once accepted as proper, may be seen to indicate lack of ontological self-sufficiency in that which they concern; from which it follows that an important part of the attempt to vindicate the questions' rationality must consist of (iii) an indication of what ontological self-sufficiency might amount to. The true nature and full scope of this defence will become clearer in due course. It may be pointed out, however, that it is a *single* three-sided defence in that (i) and (iii) both contribute basically to showing the rationality of world-contingency questions, that is, to (ii).

In the remainder of this chapter a beginning is made on the

second line of defence by considering preliminary objections to the questions which form part of the experience of contingency; or rather to one section of them, for they fall naturally into two groups which present rather different problems. Questions such as 'Why is it that anything exists?', 'Why is there anything at all?' form one group and are omitted for the time being in favour of the questions 'Why is it that the world exists?', 'Why is it that a world exists?', 'Why is there a world at all?' 'World' here naturally means 'cosmos', the total physical system as it appears to us and including ourselves. Thus it tends to exclude and is intended to exclude God or any 'Cosmos-Explaining-Being' (N. Smart's term). 'Anything' in the other questions tends rather to include God or a 'CEB' and thus to conflate the issue of a possible explanation of the cosmos with that of a possible explanation of God or a CEB. The latter is an issue which it is preferable to consider separately. To it and to questions about why anything should exist we shall return in due course.

In his careful, sustained analysis of the cosmological problem, *The Mystery of Existence*, M. K. Munitz also prefers 'Why is there a world at all?' to 'Why is there anything at all?' but for different reasons. He argues (*a*) that 'anything' could include numbers, fictional objects, and possibilities, which on the one hand each pose particular problems and on the other hand are not what arouse what he calls the sense of the mystery of existence, or in the present terminology the experience of contingency; and (*b*) that even if, to avoid this, 'anything' is restricted to natural objects, we are then faced with questions like 'Why does this chair exist?' which permit of answers in terms of natural causes and do not express the mystery of existence either.[6]

The first of these arguments is sound, but with regard to (*b*) the question 'Why does this chair exist?' *may* be interpreted as a sense of ontological shock as in the following progression: 'Why does this chair exist? Or this table? Or I myself? Or the room? Or anything?' The interpretation of the first question here as arising from an experience of contingency is illuminated by the progression but does not depend on its place in such a progression for such an interpretation. It would be impossible to interpret it in this way only if it were said to arise from an experience of contingency where 'contingency' meant 'contingency$_2$' or 'dependent on other existents in the cosmos'.

Munitz also argues that in the natural extended form of the question, 'Why does anything exist at all *rather than nothing?*', 'nothing' plays a dubious role. However, 'Why is there a world at all?' may be similarly extended. And as will be seen, his objections to 'nothing' are ill-founded.

Turning now to preliminary criticisms of 'world-contingency questions' as they may be called, it is necessary to agree first with Smart's objection to them interpreted as a request for the postulation of a logically necessary being. Such a request would indeed be nonsensical. This point is now generally agreed and will not be laboured here. It does not of course follow, as Smart rightly insists, that 'Why is there a world at all?' is nonsensical *tout court*.

That it is nonsensical may, however, be urged on other grounds. The second objection to be considered is that of positivism. Typically, world-contingency questions not only give expression to a basic puzzlement but they seek also for a resolution of this puzzlement in the form of an explanation of the world. As such they are properly speaking meaningless questions, so this objection runs, because they are in principle insoluble. The text here is Wittgenstein's *Tractatus*: 'For an answer which cannot be expressed the question too cannot be expressed. *The riddle* does not exist. If a question can be put at all, then it *can* be answered.' The thesis is that in order for a question to be genuinely significant it must be possible (*a*) to specify the methods by which an answer may be found and (*b*) to specify empirical tests that would in principle serve to determine the truth or falsity of any proposed answer. In the case of an answer to the 'Riddle of the Universe' this is impossible. Therefore an interrogative expression like 'Why is there a world at all?' is not a genuine question.[7]

Such a view no longer enjoys the influence it once did, but may be dealt with briefly. The flaw in it is the general flaw of positivism that it exalts what is appropriate in science to a position of overprivilege. The two conditions (*a*) and (*b*) may be sound criteria for the definition of a *scientific* question, but there is nothing in them to lead us to suppose that the only significant questions are scientific or empirical ones. As the positivist criterion of meaning must be rejected with regard to existence-statements, so too it must be rejected with regard to questions. As we shall see, the problem of verification is a real one, but it bears on the question of truth, not of meaning.

A cluster of three objections arises concerning 'world'. In seeking for an explanation of the world it is assumed (*a*) that the world is a whole, and it appears to be assumed (*b*) that it makes sense, and (*c*) that it is necessary, to seek an explanation 'outside' this whole. These three assumptions, so the objection runs, are indefensible. Let us, however, consider each in turn.

(i) The world/cosmos is spoken of as a whole in cosmology. And in any case, the question of the mystery of existence could be asked of any constituent of the cosmos; in the case of, for example, a chair or table we should eventually ask why it is that the energy constituting the chair exists and continues to exist. If it were claimed that the energy constituting the chair is sustained by energy elsewhere, and the claim were pressed that energy in any particular area is sustained by and sustains energy elsewhere so that we have a system of reciprocally supporting areas, then either 'system' must be taken to be totally comprehensive, in which case the objector too is thinking in terms of the world as a whole; or it must be taken as referring to a given area within a wider area or wider areas, itself containing areas of smaller dimensions, and of this a chair would be as good an example as any; in which case the objection would be not that the world is spoken of as a whole but that contingency questions are asked at all – in other words, it would belong to the third objection, (*c*), not the first, (*a*).

(ii) An outline justification of talk about a transcendent being was provided at the end of Chapter 1 and the point is explored further in Chapter 8.

(iii) The alternatives to seeking an explanation outside the world are to seek it (if it is to be sought at all) either in a part of the world, or in the relations between parts of the world, or in the world itself considered as a whole. But it is precisely contemplation of parts of the world and of their reciprocal relations, and of the concept of the world as a whole, which precipitates the sense of contingency and the quest for further explanation in the first place. Thus an empirical approach here itself impels us 'beyond' the cosmos (though it does not compel us – the argument to be expounded is not intended to be coercive).

This last point will be developed in Chapter 4, but certain comments may be added here. Thus with regard to the parts or items of the world which we know, there is, as Owen observes, 'no ground in observation, intuition, or inference' for affirming any of them to be anything other than contingent, that is to say, entities whose existence rightly puzzles us. And this is so, it should be added, even when they are specifically not abstracted from their relations with their existents.

Moreover the not totally inconceivable hypothesis 'that there *may* be an undiscovered item in the world which (unlike all the items we know) is necessary is absurd. . . . Firstly it gratuitously postulates a radical break in the fundamental character of an otherwise uniformly structured Nature. Secondly it makes the incredible assumption that though more complex entities in the evolutionary scale are non-necessary, some micro-element (hitherto undetected) is necessary.' The second of Owen's points here does not have to be accepted, but it appears considerably more plausible than C. B. Martin's suggestion that a *star* – 'a very important star, of course' – could be a necessary being in the sense of (1) a being for whose existence nothing else need exist; (2) a being that has always existed; (3) a being upon whom everything else depends for its existence. About this no more need be said than that it is in any case covered by Owen's first point. As for the meaning of 'necessary' as used by Owen, discussion of that may be postponed until later. For the moment, let 'non-contingent' suffice.[8]

With regard to the world as a whole, the inadequacy of this as a candidate for its own final explanation follows from the non-self-explanatoriness of its constituents and their interrelationship. For if the constituents of the world are contingent the world itself must be so too, for contingency concerns the *existence* of things and the *existence* of the world is nothing over and above the existence of all its constituents. Thus, though a whole may possess some qualities which its parts do not, the nature of its *existence* cannot be different. It cannot be maintained therefore that the argument from contingency errs in this respect by committing the fallacy of composition. And should any doubt still linger concerning the propriety of talking about the world as a whole, 'world' may be interpreted as a convenient abbreviation for 'any interrelated group of existents (apart from God or a

CEB if such there be)'.

It may be felt that in the preceding remarks existence has been treated illegitimately as a predicate of the world and its constituents. The objection is unfounded, however, for while existence is not a predicate of things in the sense that it affects our understanding of the *meaning* of '*x*' in '*x* exists', *whatever* the value of *x* (therefore the ontological argument fails), it must be said to be a kind of predicate in so far as the judgement '*x* exists', where the meaning of *x* is understood and where the proposition is true or is thought to be true, adds to our *knowledge*. Existence is not nothing.

Mention of 'nothing' introduces a further objection, the sixth major one in this chapter, but one which may be argued in different ways. World-contingency questions imply that there might have been nothing; but 'nothing', if it is 'intended to designate some independently conceivable possibility with which the existence of the world can be contrasted . . . must be rejected as being inherently unintelligible'. So writes Munitz in opposition to N. Smart's claim that there seems no good reason to assert that 'Nothing might have existed' is either self-contradictory or otherwise logically malformed.[9] In support of his contention Munitz reviews three lines of criticism of 'nothing' (or of the thesis that nothing might be) developed by other philosophers and then develops a contribution of his own. (There is in addition the criticism developed by C. Hartshorne, but consideration of this is reserved for another occasion, and its falseness here assumed.)

The first line of criticism is that of Bergson, according to whom the process of annihilating things in thought or conceptually cannot be carried out completely, thereby achieving the concept 'nothing', because by 'annihilation' here is meant a mental act which *replaces* one object by another.[10] The objection fails, however, because insufficient attention has been paid to the distinction between a concept and the process of conceiving. From the fact that attempts to conceive nothing coincide with there being something in one's mind, Bergson erroneously draws the conclusion that it is impossible to conceive a cessation of thought and of everything.

The second line of criticism is that of Carnap, according

to whom 'nothing' is illegitimately used in metaphysics, particularly Heidegger's, as if it were a peculiar kind of something.[11] Although the criticism of Heidegger is sound, however, the charge cannot be universalised and does not apply to the thesis developed in the present study.

The third line of criticism is that of N. L. Wilson, according to whom any attempt to state in a coherent language that there is no world is self-defeating. In his view 'the sentence "No individuals exist" . . . does not describe a possible state of affairs. If by 'conceivable' we mean 'verbalisable' (i.e. 'expressible in a synthetic sentence of an empiricistic language') then we cannot conceive of the non-existence of the world, we cannot significantly wonder why the world exists at all.'[12] Yet this is a curious argument indeed. Why in the world should anyone in the world think that from the impossibility of saying that there is no world now one can deduce the inconceivability of there having been no world now? As for difficulties in 'verbalisation', what is wrong with 'There might have been no world now' or 'It might be the case in future that there should be no individuals'?

There remains Munitz's contribution. He admits that Bergson, Carnap and Wilson do not between them get to the root of the matter, though he makes no specific criticisms, and his own attempt to do so involves an analysis of 'the world might not have been'. This statement is, he urges, either logically malformed or it contains implicit unwarranted assumptions; the implication being that since this phrase is unacceptable, so too must be its logical twins 'there might have been no world' and 'there might have been nothing'.

Munitz argues that 'might not have been' is a phrase which makes reference to a prior situation, for example 'there might not have been an explosion *if* there had been a thorough search for explosives'. 'There might not have been a world' on the other hand displays a truncated and degenerate use of the phrase. 'What would normally be the consequent of a compound [counterfactual] statement, becomes itself a complete statement.' The statement is meaningful only in a theistic context – 'had it not been for God's creative agency, there would not have been a world'. Outside this context it is nonsense; within it it begs the question.[13]

'Outside this context it is nonsense.' Not so. It may be

contended that it is capable of two significant interpretations outside the theistic context.

It is arguable that 'the world exists' is logically necessary for us who are in it. The necessity is, however, 'consequential' only.[14] 'It is (tenseless 'is') necessary that there be (tenseless 'be') a world for us to be in at all and in which we can affirm logical necessity' is not itself logically necessary. But if not, what is the alternative? On non-theistic premises, or better 'non-religious' premises in order to exclude the possibility of Nirvana or some other transcendent alternative existing, only nothing remains. Thus the first non-theistic interpretation of 'The world might not have been' is its equation with the logical contingency of the above-mentioned proposition.

The second interpretation is its equation with the logical contingency of 'The world must continue to be', where the verbs are tensed. Granted that this proposition is not logically necessary, then *if* the world had not continued to be, there would have been no world; that is to say, no world now. In which case, again on the agreed non-religious premises, the only conceivable alternative is nothing.

In both cases 'nothing' as a coherent concept is indeed strictly deducible from the logical contingency of the propositions instanced.

That the difference between the two interpretations is of some moment will become apparent in Chapter 4.

A seventh objection, to which we now turn, is that world-contingency questions like 'Why is there a world at all?' imply that the world must have had an origin in the sense of a temporal beginning. Clearly, however, the questions carry no such implication. They refer to every moment of the existence of the cosmos, not to a temporal origin which it may or may not have had. This is now generally agreed and was apparent already to Aquinas.

An eighth objection is that world-contingency questions imply that there *must be* a reason or explanation for the world's existence, which is a gratuitous assumption, an unwarranted elevating of the principle of sufficient reason from a scientific postulate to a metaphysical law. We should ask rather '*Is* there a reason for the world's existence?'[15]

This proposal has the merit of caution, but 'Is there a reason

for the world's existence?' is altogether too abstractly speculative to represent the *experience* of contingency which is the
starting-point of the present discussion. That experience naturally gives rise to existential why-questions which are indeed
speculative but speculative and more, or 'involvedly' speculative. It is preferable therefore to retain 'Why is there a world
at all?' and related world-contingency questions, though naturally bearing in mind that there may be no answer to them in
terms of a reason for the world's existence. The question of the
status of the principle of sufficient reason is one which will be
taken up in due course.

So much for initial objections. With regard to these eight at
least it may be concluded that, whatever the eventual outcome,
world-contingency questions are properly formulated questions which it is legitimate to ask. Other objections will be discussed later. For the moment it is assumed that the questions
are in order. Is it possible to provide a satisfactory answer to
them? First, two different approaches will be considered which
both answer in the affirmative. Finally, an alternative view is
developed.

3 Rival Uses of Contingency

(i) *Metaphysical Intuitionism*

A number of thinkers, including I. Trethowan, M. Pontifex and
H. D. Lewis, and to some extent E. L. Mascall and A. Farrer,
have canvassed the possibility of taking a putative metaphysical
intuition or apprehension of the source of being as a valid basis
for belief in God. To quote Lewis: 'We seem to see that in the
last resort the world just could not exist by some extraordinary
chance or just happen . . . all that we encounter points to a Reality which is complete and self-contained and which is the ultimate ground or condition of all the conditioned, limited reality
we find ourselves and the world around us to be.'[1] We should,
he urges, adopt Trethowan's shrewd advice to go on looking 'at
what being stands for until it breaks into finite and infinite'.
This 'one leap of thought in which finite and infinite are equally
present and which cannot be broken up into steps which we
may negotiate one by one' is the ground of our belief. The mis-
take of the traditional arguments, including the cosmological
argument, is in 'trying to break into a series of steps what is in
fact one insight'.[2] The basis of belief is thus an apprehension of
God and the world in the 'cosmological relationship' (Farrer),
an 'intuition' of God (Lewis) or, as Mascall says, a 'contuition'.
The sense of contingency as it has been briefly delineated here
becomes a sense of 'contingency' in an explicitly theological
sense, that is to say, it deepens into a feeling of dependence, yet
'not just a feeling . . . but a conviction or insight, a sense that
something must be, a cognition in more technical terms'.[3]

There is no question in all this of using the experience of contingency as a basis for an inference of any kind to God. Lewis's
reference to the traditional arguments has just been noted.

Similarly, Mascall writes:

> In rising to a conviction of God's existence from finite beings,
> we do not . . . merely perceive the existence of these things by
> the senses and then, by a subsequent process of purely logical
> deduction, arrive at an intellectual acceptance of the prop-
> osition 'God exists'. On the contrary, if our mind . . . is able
> freely to fulfil its proper function of apprehending finite
> beings as they really are, it will, in the very act by which it ap-
> prehends them, be capable of penetrating to the ontological
> depths of their nature so as to know them as the creatures of
> God.

Again we read: 'The existence of God is not inferred by a logical
process but apprehended in a cognitive act.'[4]

This taking exception to inference or argument as a means of
validating belief in God is familiar from Chapter 1, and the
present position is exposed to the criticisms which were there
levelled at the notion of self-authenticating religious experience. For although the advocates of metaphysical intuitions
emphasise self-authenticating 'insight' or 'cognition', this is as
epistemologically precarious as the kinds of experience discussed previously. It will not do to beg the question as to
whether one's intuitions are trustworthy by labelling them
'insights' or 'disclosures' or 'apprehensions', still less 'cog-
nitions'. Once again the problem of rival intuitions arises –
Lewis's experience of contingency involves God, Munitz's does
not. What is the risk run by either of hoodwinking himself, and
how are they or how is anyone else to decide the issue? The
appeal to self-authentication will no more do here than elsewhere. *Some* kind of *argument* from 'contingency' in a non-
theological sense is called for rather than appeal to an experience of 'contingency' in a question-begging sense.

(ii) *A Traditional or 'Hard' Cosmological Approach*

Such an argument receives a measure of support from Mascall
which remains to be mentioned and is developed in detail by
Owen in chap. 4 of his *The Christian Knowledge of God*.

In *He Who Is*, Mascall writes as follows:

> The arguments for the existence of God are not fallacious,

and to anyone who understands what they are about and is capable of following them they can carry complete conviction. Nor are they unnecessary, for without them – or at least without some equivalent consideration such as Garrigou-Lagrange's one general proof – our belief will not be explicitly rational. But their real value is in stimulating the mind to examine finite beings with such attention and understanding that it grasps them in their true ontological nature as dependent upon God, and so grasp God's existence as their Creator.[5]

Here Mascall appears to lay stress on both experience and argument. The experience is necessary but the argument is valid and can act as a rational justification.

This position is upheld in Mascall's subsequent *Existence and Analogy*, but an aura of ambivalence is introduced:

I must make it plain that the remarks in which I have just been indulging . . . are not to be considered as an argument for the existence of God. Whether we describe the cosmological approach itself as an argument depends mainly on how the word 'argument' is defined. Its crux consists not in a process of logical deduction but in an apprehension, namely the apprehension of finite beings as effect implying (or, better, manifesting) a transcendent cause. [Nevertheless, he urges, argument has a place, and can indeed] convince us that such apprehension, when it has occurred, is not to be dismissed as an illusion.[6]

This is not altogether satisfactory. Stress is laid on the apprehension of finite beings as effect manifesting a transcendent cause, that is to say, on a form of religious experience$_1$. Now the difficulties of religious experience$_1$ as the basis of an argument have already been touched on in Chapter 1; and by saying here that he is not presenting an argument for the existence of God, Mascall implies that argument convinces only those who have had the experience. The question thus arises whether the argument offered in justification of the metaphysical apprehension can in fact justify without begging the question.

And in a third work, *Words and Images*, Mascall states explicitly that it cannot. As defended by some scholastics, Aquinas's Five Ways have the form of a hypothetical constructive syllogism. Thus the Third Way reads: If there exists a contingent being there must exist a necessary being. But there do exist contingent beings. Therefore there exists a necessary being, and 'this all men speak of as God'. The difficulty which such apologists face, says Mascall, is 'how to prove the truth of the major premise without already begging the conclusion, and I for one cannot see how this can be done'. He then draws attention approvingly to the different approach represented by Farrer, Pontifex and Trethowan where the function of the arguments is to direct the mind to certain aspects of existents, otherwise easily overlooked, from which the existence of God can be seen 'without a discursive process'. It is not denied, he continues, that 'there is a great deal to be done in the way of argument and discussion', but the purpose of such argument is to engineer an apprehension, an apprehension not of 'the-creature-without-God' nor of 'God-without-the-creature', but of 'the-creature-deriving-being-from-God and God-as-the-creative-ground-of-the-creature:God-and-the-creature-in-the-cosmological-relation'. Thus Mascall's final emphasis is on that intuition or contuition which was criticised above. (The emphasis reappears in his subsequent Gifford Lectures, despite hints at a possible harmony of contuition and inference.[7])

The shift of emphasis here is entirely unfortunate. A question-begging argument is of little value, but Mascall's initial emphasis on both experience and argument could have been saved without resorting to this dubious means. In the passage quoted from *Existence and Analogy*, Mascall emphasises the apprehension of finite beings as effects manifesting a transcendent cause. Yet in place of 'manifesting' he first writes 'implying' and the whole phrase is a modification of Pontifex's phrase 'effect-implying-cause'.[8] Now if emphasis is laid on the apprehension of an effect *implying* a cause, or a transcendent cause (and on 'effect' as *effect* only if the implication is upheld), then there exists the possibility of rationally assessing the nature and strength of the implication and of developing it in the form of an argument without begging the question. For while the apprehension of an effect manifesting a transcendent cause is a form of religious experience₁, the apprehension of an effect implying such a cause is a form of religious experience$_2$. In itself it is a non-religious experience susceptible of religious reinterpretation. There is thus no question of God appearing in the basis of the argument.

The possibility of such an argument has been developed in detail by Owen. His defence of the argument from contingency is a careful and thorough piece of work from which a central core only is here extracted. The present discussion has already covered several topics dealt with by him and attention will be drawn to others subsequently.

Owen takes as his starting-point the contingency of the world in the fourth sense of 'contingency', meaning that the world 'does not contain within itself a power of inevitable existence', so that of anything around us it may significantly be asked why it exists at all or why it should be rather than not be, and argues that *if* we are to have a sufficient reason for or explanation of the world, we must proceed beyond all finite causes and postulate the existence of a necessary being as the first cause of all that is ('first', that is, in the order of being, not of time). This argument, he urges, is valid but *hypothetical*, for it presupposes acceptance of the principle of sufficient reason, a principle which is neither self-evident nor demonstrable.[9] This is a point which will be considered later. Accepting the principle for the moment, let us focus on the other main feature of his argument, the concept of a necessary being or God.

To say that God's existence is necessary, or that he is 'self-existent', is to say that 'in him essence and existence (*what* he is and *that* he is) are identical. If we could see his essence, or nature, we should simultaneously see it as pervaded by a power of inevitable existence.' Yet in our present states the idea of self-existent being is bound to be incomprehensible, a 'total mystery' of which we cannot form even a faintly appropriate analogy. Yet to say that it is imcomprehensible is not to say that it is self-contradictory. 'It would be self-contradictory only if God were a magnified man to whom the attribute of necessity is arbitrarily affixed, or if his existence were an unqualified X. But existence is not a genus which God shares with men; it is an activity (in itself, inevitably, indefinable) that is diversely structured; and the divine structure is qualitatively different from its human copies.'[10]

It may have been noticed that in the original account of Owen's argument what is reached in the conclusion is not the personal God of religion but a necessary being. Owen later justifies the identification of the two as follows:

> God's personality is deducible from the conclusion of the cosmological argument in two main ways.
>
> Firstly, to say that God is self-existent is to say that his nature is simply 'to be'. His essence, so far from circumscribing existence, totally exhausts it. But it is inherent in any material entity to exclude other entities, and to constitute with them parts of a whole. Hence God must be non-material or spiritual. Furthermore, if his essence is coincident with existence it must include every aspect of spiritual being – intelligence, will, and love cohering in a unique Subject.
>
> Secondly, if God creates the world *ex nihilo* he must contain within himself in some mode every perfection which the world contains. In this case it is self-evident that the cause must contain as much reality as its effects; for the effects owe their *total* being to the *immediate* effects of the cause. Therefore God must possess every element in human spirituality (or personality) *formaliter et eminentius*.[11]

This move from necessary being to personal God is a first source of unease regarding Owen's position. What does it *mean* to say that God's essence totally exhausts existence, or 'existence *as such*', as he elsewhere puts it?[12] Again, are non-materiality and spirituality equivalent? We are naturally inclined to think so, but can we say that non-materiality entails spirituality? Further, even if we can, if God's essence includes *every* aspect of spiritual being, why restrict these aspects to positive, admirable ones like intelligence, will and love? Owen's first deduction (*deduction*, no less) of God's personality from the conclusion of the cosmological argument is thus a source of considerable unease.

As for the second, we are told that it is 'self-evident' that in the case of the relation between necessary being and the world, the cause must contain as much reality as its effects. Yet it is far from self-evident. Owen states in a footnote that this inference should be distinguished from the view that every effect is like its cause – a view which is dubious in the case of ordinary causes, and in any case God is not an ordinary cause – but the distinction is not obvious; and it is not clear why the fact that in the case of the cosmological relation the effects owe their *total* being to the *immediate* effects of the cause should be considered decisive. Again, even if these difficulties are overcome, why say only that God must contain in some mode every *perfection* which the world contains? Quite apart from the point that all such perfections may not be compossible in one subject.

In addition, Owen begins his second deduction by saying 'if God creates the world *ex nihilo* . . .'. But 'God' here should mean 'necessary being' only, not 'personal necessary being', for the purpose of the argument is to deduce the latter from the former. If 'God' does mean 'necessary being', however, what sense does it make to say 'God creates'? As Owen goes on to point out, we cannot think of a creative cause except in terms that are fully personal, but in that case to write 'creates' here is to assume that the cosmological relation between the world and a necessary being or first cause is a relation of creation. Does it have to be? That would be a difficult thesis to sustain. Admittedly, alternatives are hard to come by – perhaps impossible. But then again the relation is *ex hypothesi* unique, so that is not an insuperable obstacle. In any event it is a position for which Owen offers no support. All this amounts to a most serious difficulty in an argument which is alleged, given the principle of sufficient reason, to be coercive.

Thus the transition in Owen's argument from necessary being to personal God is a source of grave suspicion. For all one might know from adhering strictly to the argument itself, the necessary being could be virtually anything. It would be a logical stop-card but one that bore no apprehensible markings; a necessary-being-shaped blank.

With regard to the nature of this logical stop-card too, objections may be raised. Its necessity is said to lie in the fact that its essence and existence coincide. But the coincidence of essence and existence in the divine being is frequently adduced as a basis for the ontological argument. Owen explicitly rejects this argument and asserts that God's necessity is not logical necessity – but, he significantly adds, not logical necessity 'for human minds'.[13] Apparently, therefore, he here follows Aquinas in claiming that while the logical necessity of the divine existence is for ever veiled from our finite minds, it is apparent to God himself. Could we but penetrate to knowledge of his nature we too should apprehend this logical necessity.

Now this is a disturbing doctrine. It is true, as has been indicated, that certain existential propositions are in a sense necessary – 'I exist' or 'The world exists' as uttered by someone – yet this necessity is consequential. Given my existence 'I exist' as uttered by me is necessarily true, but it is not logically necessary that I should have been 'given' or that I should continue to be 'given'. Now in the case of God much more may be claimed. Given his existence at any moment, then it is logically necessary that he should continue to exist and that he should never have not existed – and if this were Owen's contention there would be nothing to which to take exception. That it is his contention, however, remains doubtful. For according to it there is no sense in which the divine necessity is logical necessity for God but not for us. Again, it is not clear that it represents the coincidence of essence and existence in the divine nature, for does not the doctrine that essence and existence coincide entail that essence entails existence as in the ontological argument and thus that 'God exists' is after all, ultimately, logically necessary, that it is logically necessary that God be 'given'?

Moreover other passages in Owen indicate that this last view is the one he holds, for example: 'God is not intelligible . . . to *us*. His essence remains a complete mystery. Hence the ontological argument is bound to fail. Because we do not have a "clear and distinct" idea of God's essence we cannot deduce from it that he exists. If we did have this idea we should not need the proof; for we should then see his existence and his essence in their pure identity.' His claim here is that we should not need the proof, not that the proof would be invalid. Yet this will not do. 'To say that although God's existence is self-evident in itself it is not to us is to say that it *is* self-evident in itself, and the error lies here. It is not our ignorance that is the obstacle to explaining God's existence by his nature [that is, to making the ontological argument work and to attributing, ultimately, logical necessity to 'God exists'], but the logical character of the concept of existence.'[14] Owen argues that the divine mode of existence is utterly without analogy, but even if this be accepted (and it need not be, as will be seen) it must not be construed as giving us logical licence to do what we will with the concept of existence, and certainly not to treat it in the above-mentioned manner. Indeed, if we do treat it in this way, in what recognisable sense are we still talking about '*existence*'? To proceed thus is to lay oneself open to Flew's salutary 'death by a thousand qualifications' charge.

According to Mascall, 'if God exists, we can, with St Thomas, identify his essence with his act of existing and say that it is his essence to exist; but until we know that he exists all that we can say is that *if* he exists this identification can be made'.[15] Now to make the identification conditional upon his existence is to identify his essence with his *continued* existence rather than with his existence *tout court*, with his existing *at all*. In this sense the doctrine of the coincidence of essence and existence is ambiguous. The point here, however, is that Owen does not operate in terms of such an ambiguity – which is a pity, for the former is consonant with his cosmological argument and the latter with his rejection of the ontological argument – but with a duality of standpoint, God's and ours, which is illegitimately said to affect the question of the logical necessity of 'God exists'. Yet at the root of this error is perhaps the fact that the verbal identity of the two different doctrines of the coincidence of essence and existence beguiles the unsuspecting person who accepts the legitimate doctrine (the identification of essence with continued existence) to attempt the impossible task of reconciling this with a consequence flowing from the other, illegitimate doctrine, namely the consequence that 'God exists' must (ultimately) be logically necessary.

Here then are two suggested lines of criticism of Owen's argument, directed basically at his conclusion and not at the approach in general. The first suggests that his conclusion is rather barren, and this is the one to which most weight is attached here. The second is that his conclusion is incoherent, but this may be avoided by modifying the conclusion to some extent.

Nevertheless, in view of the objections raised against both Owen and Mascall, chosen as typifying two rival and influential approaches, it is worth asking whether there is any possibility of formulating an argument from contingency which is not question-begging and which leads to a coherent concept of God – which leads indeed to the God of religion. In the following chapter it is suggested that there may be.

4 A 'Soft' Cosmological Approach

It was argued in Chapter 2 that world-contingency questions are, for all that there was offered to the contrary, legitimate questions requesting an explanation of the cosmos in terms of something other than the cosmos or a part of the cosmos, that is to say, requesting what may be called a 'non-natural' explanation of the cosmos.

Yet if the questions are indeed to be accepted as legitimate and rational, it is necessary to inquire into and to be clear about their implications. What are their presuppositions? It is arguable that the basic presupposition is that the world in some way lacks ontological self-sufficiency. For the questions are directed at the world's *existence*. Now since its existence calls for explanation, it would seem to follow that the nature of this existence must in some way point beyond itself to some kind of putative *explicans*, the nature of whose existence must differ in kind from that of the world otherwise there results a vicious infinite regress. And the difference between the two kinds of existence may be brought out by labelling the one self-sufficient and the other not (the nature of the distinction to be elaborated later). Thus, if this line of reasoning be sound, acceptance of the full rationality of world-contingency questions implies the identification of contingency$_5$ with contingency$_4$. Henceforth, therefore, wherever 'contingency' occurs in the context of acceptance, even if only provisional, of the questions' rationality, it should be interpreted as 'contingency$_4$/contingency$_5$'.

The point about an infinite regress may be developed in connection with a further aspect of the problem of the rationality of world-contingency questions. Typically, the questions are requests for an ultimate explanation, an explanation beyond which it is impossible to go. It is indeed a feature of the questions that if it could be shown that the notion of a *final* non-natural explanation is incoherent, they would cease to be asked seriously; and this would be so even if *some* kind of explanation of the cosmos could be suggested. That is to say, if such an explanation itself stood in need of explanation, and so on, and if a means of ending the regress were held to be truly inconceivable, then even if one still experienced some sense of ontological shock, rationally one would have to force oneself to accept the fact of the world's existence as just the way things are. 'Why is there a world at all?' and related questions could be reinterpreted so as to have a limited formal validity (analogous, as will be seen, to the limited formal validity of 'Why is there a God?'), but as normally interpreted would have to be rejected as leading to the postulation of an infinity of unverifiable entities, each as contingent (senses 5 and 4) as its predecessor, and consequently as unsatisfactorily explanatory.

The questions are thus at root Janus-questions, performing the functions both of seeking an explanation of the cosmos and of seeking a non-natural explanatory terminus; the two being linked in that, without an explanatory terminus, contingency (senses 5 and 4), the *explicandum*, is not finally eradicated. And the full rationality of the former function depends on the possibility of the success of the latter. Unless both functions are satisfied, or are thought to be capable of being satisfied, the questions should fizzle out. (The further support which this conclusion requires is supplied in subsequent discussion.)

Now the notion of a logically necessary being would, if coherent, provide an excellent non-natural explanatory terminus; for its existence could no more be questioned than can the four-sidedness of a square. Hence no doubt the appeal to such a being by advocates of arguments from contingency. And once the notion of such a being is rejected, the prospect of a non-natural explanatory terminus begins to appear dubious, for what is there to prevent the existence of whatever candidate is suggested being questioned?

More basically, however, the very notion of an explanatory terminus is sometimes impugned. It is necessary therefore to examine this notion first before proceeding to discuss its possible theological application and to explore the notion of an ontologically self-sufficient being.

In any event it may be concluded for the present that if world-contingency questions are to be accepted as fully rational, in the sense of being both formally valid and worth pursuing, then the notion of a non-natural explanatory terminus must be acceptable, and the notion of an ontologically self-sufficient being be conceivable which would be capable of filling that role. Conversely, if these conditions cannot be fulfilled the questions become intellectually (and most certainly theologically) emasculated, patient of a restricted and largely sterile reinterpretation only (again as will be seen below).

(i)

C. B. Martin has usefully distinguished three kinds of explanation, historical, purposive and theoretical; and the notion of an explanatory terminus may be fruitfully explored via this distinction.

(1) What he calls 'historical' explanation is an explanation involving a causal series; for example, 'B is the parent of A, C is the parent of B, D is the parent of C', etc.; or 'Why did the glass fall?' 'Because the table moved', 'Why did the table move?' 'Because the house shook', etc. To such a series of answers there is no limit or terminus (unless it be a putative beginning of the world).

(2) Explanation in terms of purpose, reason or motive, on the other hand (the differences between these three are of no immediate relevance), can*not* proceed without limit. Martin suggests the following conversation: 'Why did you smash the glass?' 'Because I wanted to.' 'Why did you want to?' 'Because I wanted to attract the waiter's attention.' 'Why?' 'Because I was hungry and wanted him to bring food.' This conversation might be developed still further as follows. 'Why?' 'Because I wanted to live – and indeed still do.' 'Why?' 'I just do. Things are such, and I am such, that I just do.' End of explanation.

According to Martin, 'the purposive kind of explanation does not explain (as it may seem to do) by relating the falling glass event to some sort of mental event of wanting or purposing. If it did, it would not be different from the causal kind of explanation.' This is acceptable in so far as it militates against reducing purposive to causal explanation, but unacceptable in so far as it clashes with the judgement that 'if we mention a *future* state which is aimed at, then we can refer to the *present* or *past state of aiming*, that is, the present or past intention to achieve that future state. So for every teleological explanation there could be a parallel explanation in terms of the causal efficacy of the intention.' That is a matter which cannot be pursued here, however; further support for Shaffer's conclusion will be found in the relevant sections of his book.[1]

(3) 'Theoretical explanation of a course of events may have higher and higher levels of generality and abstractness. "Why did the glass break?" "It is fragile." This explanation involves a generalisation open to non-technical observation. "Why is it fragile?" "The molecular structure is [physical or technical description]." "Why is the molecular structure this way?" "The atomic [subatomic, subsubatomic]. . . ."

'I want very much to say that explanation of this sort must stop somewhere. And I want to say that the stopping is not merely a practical or arbitrary device', writes Martin.

What could constitute a non-arbitrary stopping-place? An ultimate or basic law of nature, 'one that would hold at all times and places and would not be deducible from any other law of nature of greater abstractness or generality'. Such a law would be logically contingent and therefore might conceivably have been other, but 'to ask of an account of how the world is as it is that it should be true by logical necessity is to ask the logically impossible'.

Nevertheless the desire to ask this is, Martin concedes, to some degree understandable, and he illustrates the point with a quotation which may profitably be reproduced in full:

If a law is really a basic one, any request for an explanation of it is self-contradictory. To explain a law is to place it in a context or network of wider and more inclusive laws; a basic law is by definition one of which this cannot be done. . . . Like so many others, this point may seem logically compelling but psychologically unsatisfying. Having heard the above argument, one may still feel inclined to ask, 'Why are the basic uniformities of the universe the way they are, and not some other way? Why should we have just *these* laws rather than other ones? I want an *explanation* of why they are as they are.'

I must confess here, as an autobiographical remark, that I

cannot help sharing this feeling; I want to ask why the laws of nature, being contingent, are as they are, even though I cannot conceive of what an explanation of this would be like, and even though by my own argument above the request for such an explanation is self-contradictory.

Martin comments: 'When we come to a place where higher-level explanation stops (some law in physics that we take rightly or wrongly to be basic) . . . we may be content to say that no further explanation is needed, or we may (it is a matter of temperament) feel dissatisfied with a bare contingency.'[2]

Now this analysis of types of explanation is broadly speaking acceptable. Thus the notion of an explanatory terminus is plausible in the context both of purposive explanation and of theoretical explanation. How then is the metaphysical quest for explanation expressed by questions like 'Why is there a world at all?' related to these kinds of explanation?

It is not of course a request for a historical causal explanation. The possibility of there being no explanatory terminus in that context is thus of no immediate relevance.

The metaphysical quest is *not* a request for a purposive explanation. This must be stated explicitly here, briefly but emphatically, in order to counter an accusation such as the following, levelled by Flew at N. Smart, that 'it is to satisfy a demand for explanation in distinctively personal terms that the take-off is made into a scientifically redundant dimension'.[3] Whatever the outcome of the quest, the interpretation of its nature in these terms is thoroughly erroneous. The metaphysical quest for an explanation of the world's existence is in the first instance simply a request for an *explanation*, for light to be shed on a dark puzzle, for illumination of something opaque to the intellect. The basic requirement is that the explanation explain, not that it be personal, or spiritual. If the intellectual motivation be accompanied by, or even spring from, a religious or spiritual motivation, so be it. The intellectual thrusts and parries of argument nevertheless call for evaluation in their own right and in their own terms.

If then a satisfactory explanation should be found it may prove to be purposive, but this is not necessarily envisaged at the outset. It may prove to be theoretical, or both purposive and theoretical, since in both cases the notion of an explanatory terminus is acceptable. It may, however, prove to be an explanation of some other kind, for there is no reason why this threefold analysis of the kinds of explanation should necessarily be exhaustive, or why the notion of an explanatory terminus should not be acceptable with regard to another kind of explanation.

Yet one thing is clear. The metaphysical quest is a request for a non-natural explanation – for the *explicandum* is nothing less than the natural world itself. And in the possibility of a non-natural explanation lies the possibility of proceeding beyond the position taken up by Hospers. Hospers's position may be summed up as follows: 'Why *these* laws rather than others?' is a silly question, for if there is to be a world at all it must be this rather than that, whatever the character of 'this', and consequently the scandal of particularity expressed by the question is no real scandal. Such a view clearly presupposes, however, the existence of the world, and if this may legitimately be questioned, it could follow that underlying each puzzle giving rise to a request for theoretical or indeed causal explanation of the kind offered by science is a puzzle giving rise to a request for an explanation of another kind. And the request would find expression (crudely) not in 'Why *these* laws?' but in 'Why that to which the laws apply?', or world-contingency questions. Moreover it follows that a basic law of the cosmos could supply only a scientific or natural theoretical explanatory terminus, not a theoretical explanatory terminus *tout court*. Given the legitimacy of questioning the existence of the world there could be a non-natural theoretical explanatory terminus, or in any event a non-natural explanatory terminus.

'Given the legitimacy of questioning the existence of the world.' This legitimacy has been defended in the face of several objections, but the crucial move remains to be made. It is that of pointing to an ambiguity in world-contingency questions and exploiting it in support of the suggestion that the 'normal' interpretation is not the most fruitful one; that it may well not be the one which most accurately expresses that experience of contingency which has been a nerve in previous attempts to defend an argument from contingency; and that in a sense remaining to be clarified it is not the most fully rational one.

The three world-contingency questions mentioned in Chapter 2, 'Why is it that the world exists?', 'Why is it that a world exists?', 'Why is there a world at all?', are each susceptible of two interpretations. The distinction between them is of fundamental importance yet passes unnoticed as such in the literature. Stated in a nutshell it is the distinction between the questions as taken to be significantly tensed and the questions as taken to be tenseless. If 'is' and 'exists' in these questions are taken to be *tensed*, the questions properly speaking express puzzlement at the fact of ontological *continuance*. Only if the verbs are *tenseless* do the questions properly express puzzlement at the fact of the world's existing *at all*.

The nature and significance of this distinction will become clearer as the argument proceeds. It is perhaps as well to note, however, that the three questions are not completely equivalent even when all are explicitly given either a tensed or a tenseless interpretation. It is helpful to number the six possibilities:

(1) why is it that the world exists? (tensed)
(2) Why is it that the world exists? (tenseless)
(3) Why is it that a world exists? (tensed)
(4) Why is it that a world exists? (tenseless)
(5) Why is there a world at all? (tensed)
(6) Why is there a world at all? (tenseless)

Taking the tensed versions only for the moment, they may be expounded briefly as follows:

(1) Why is it that the world as we know it exists and goes on existing?
(3) As above, but with the added implication that the question would be asked of all other worlds that might conceivably exist in place of the one we know, provided that they were similar to it in the important aspect that to ask this question of them was not nonsensical or silly.
(5) As (3).

Thus there is a distinction between (1) on the one hand and (3) and (5) on the other. However, it is of no immediate importance for the argument to be developed and we may concentrate on (1). For when (3) and (5) are asked, what the questioner has in mind is a world that *is* sufficiently similar to the present world to generate the puzzle expressed in (1). Nevertheless, although the distinction does not affect the course of the subsequent argument, it is worth making briefly for the sake of absolute clarity.

With regard to the tenseless questions it is convenient to postpone consideration of them until the next section of this chapter when they may be interpreted by contrast with their tensed counterparts, of which by then a clearer and comprehensive picture will be available. The immediate task must be to give as full an initial indication as possible of the puzzle lying at the heart of the tensed questions.

It was referred to in passing as the puzzle of 'ontological continuance'. It is the puzzle that the world should be (tensed 'be') and should continue on its way. Why is it that the world continues? What is there about it which makes it keep going?

It might be felt that in reply appeal should be made to the law of the conservation of energy, for example; but this only describes the *explicandum*, it does not explain it.

Or in so far as the present may be said to be caused by the past and to cause the future, it might be felt that appeal should be made to the law of causality; but this too is unsatisfactory in that it seems to involve a strained extension of what 'cause' means. 'Causation, as commonly understood, relates to change within the already existent.' 'A substance or motion . . . is causal only if it is continued into a different motion. Thus there is no causality in the continuance without change of the same motion. . . . Causality would become an insignificant notion if it could be applied with this looseness.'[4] Yet according to the view in which appeal is made to the law of causality, a temporal antecedent, no matter of what kind, not only acts as a cause and affects, but also and more importantly *effects*, a temporal successor, even in the sense of itself at a later instant. Thus dissatisfaction with the natural theoretical type of explanation (in this case involving the law of causality) as a solution to the puzzle of ontological continuance springs from dissatisfaction with the causal type of explanation involving particular instantiations of the law of causality. Within its terms of reference causal explanation explains adequately, but is it the whole story? If we explain an effect in terms of a cause or causes, have we *fully* explained its existence? The suggestion here is that we have not.

If this view be accepted, it follows that a cosmological-type argument based upon it is not exposed to the objection illustrated by P. Edwards's story of a group of five Eskimos standing on the corner of Sixth Avenue and 50th Street. Each Eskimo is there for a different reason and a different explanation is accordingly supplied for the presence of each. It is then absurd to ask, 'All right, but what about the group as a whole; why is *it* in New York?' My contention, however, is that though causal explanation of any one thing may be adequate to account for it causally, it is inadequate to account for it completely, and that this is true of any causal or indeed theoretical explanation of anything in the world. Only if the causal or theoretical account were completely adequate would the objection hold. And so too with regard to purposive explanation. This may be adequate within its own terms, but the continued existence of purposing selves remains unexplained in these terms.[5]

Just as there seems to be nothing about causality which at the present time ensures the continued existence of the world in the future, so too the continued existence of the world in a given duration of time in the past does not seem to have been ensured by its state prior to that duration. Yet despite this lack of 'ensurance', it continued. By the principle of sufficient reason a request for further explanation for this would appear to be in order.

The puzzle which an attempt is being made here to indicate is *not* that there is (tenseless 'is') a world at all. That is another issue altogether. It concerns rather the mode of the world's continued existence. This cannot be overemphasised, for it is the crux of the whole chapter.

Yet the nature of the puzzle is difficult to formulate satisfactorily, for the awareness (or putative apprehension) of it is elusive. We know that the world has a long history. We anticipate it lasting indefinitely. Yet at times at least this seems far from self-explanatory. It is opaque to our understanding, in that although the world apparently proceeds under its own steam, it is not self-evident that the process of generating this steam is self-sufficient. The sense of ontological shock at there being and continuing to be a world involves an intimation of a certain ontological precariousness in the experienced flow from present to present. The apparent self-sustenance of the energy constituting the cosmos becomes a source of intellectual disquietude. On the basis of our experience of the world we seem to know that it will continue, yet also on the basis of our experience of the world we fail to see why it should. Thus on this view the experience of contingency$_5$ is founded in a dim sense of an *ever-present* threat of non-being (as opposed to being founded in a vaguely, or indeed clearly, formulated conception that there might *have been* nothing – a conception which connects rather with the tenseless interpretation of world-contingency questions); and that when the threat is consciously realised, the experience modulates into an experience of contingency$_4$.

Again, on this view the logical contingency of 'The world exists' (tensed 'exists'), the fact that in point of logic it is easily conceivable that the world should simply cease, is a reflection of the world's factual contingency. The linguistic propriety of 'The world does not cease to exist; why not?' faithfully represents a felt factual propriety. And it is to a considerable extent on the basis of this experience that the obvious and important counter-argument, 'It is conceivable that the world should simply cease, but there is no obvious reason why it should, therefore to seek a reason for its not doing so is gratuitous', is deemed inadequate.

Yet this 'intuition', as some might wish to call it, may be defended in a way that intuitions falling in the category of religious experience$_1$ cannot. Therefore there is no question here of a kind of contingency-intuitionism. Rejection of the above counter-argument may be sustained by reference to the three-sided defence anticipated in Chapter 2. Thus it may be urged:

(*a*) That the counter-argument runs counter to that form of the experience of contingency which does not include world-contingency questions, and the nature of which is such as to justify a certain trust in its validity (as was argued in Chapter 2.)

(*b*) That by conceding the conceivability of the world's ceasing to exist, it does not dispute the right in principle to ask for a reason for the world's continued existence, and that in the absence of further argument to show that such a question is silly, what it in effect does is subordinate the principle of sufficient reason to the law of parsimony – which is in principle a questionable procedure; for no explanation of the world's continuing to be is offered (since the need for explanation is denied), its continued existence is simply accepted, and if this acceptance may sensibly be questioned, then it (the acceptance) faces the charge of involving a refusal to press the question 'why?' to its legitimate limit – a refusal which cannot be brooked by supporters of the principle of sufficient reason.

(c) That if it is possible to present a coherent non-natural explanation of the alleged puzzle of ontological continuance and at the same time provide a non-natural explanatory terminus, this will go some way towards both justifying adherence to the principle of sufficient reason in this case, and justifying belief that there is a puzzle at all by contrasting the putative *explicandum* with its *explicans* and saying: Look, that is what explains what is supposed to be a puzzle, and that is how it explains it; can you not now see that there is a puzzle after all?

Let us now take these three points in turn.

With regard to (a) it remains only to consider the possible objection that since consciousness is atomic, i.e. proceeding in 'drops' rather than in durationless instants of experience, putative apprehension of ontological continuance and insight into its precariousness is worthless because we do not apprehend it anyway – it belongs to sub-threshold durations and concerns the sub-threshold succession of instants of time. This objection may be met in part by pointing out that the move from one specious present to the next affords the possibility of insight into ontological precariousness; and in part by claiming that there is intellectual apprehension of ontological continuance and (continuous) temporal passage even if no direct awareness.

Much has already been offered both in Chapter 2 and in the present chapter by way of substantiation of (b), yet remaining to be considered is the notable issue of the principle of sufficient reason. This will be taken up in section (iii) of this chapter.

It may be conceded, however, that without the considerations adduced in Chapter 5 below for identifying a putative CEB with the God of religion, and without others adduced in Chapters 6 and 10, there is a strong temptation to disregard in this case the natural precedence of the principle of sufficient reason over Occam's razor. Yet it would not necessarily be fully rational to do so, and it is certainly not rational in the initial stages of inquiry and against the background of the apparently respectable form of the experience of contingency. (Though if, contrary to what is urged below, an infinite series of CEBs were found to be necessary in order to provide a satisfactory explanation, then perhaps it would indeed be rational to disregard the natural subservience of Occam's razor to the principle of sufficient reason, and to place them on an equal footing with a resulting deadlock, or even to reverse their positions.)

It might be argued that although the principle of sufficient reason takes precedence over Occam's razor, it does not take precedence over Occam's razor combined with the Stratonician principle, and that this is the combination which it faces here. Stratonician atheism is defended of course by Flew, and the Stratonician principle may be formulated as the principle that 'all qualities observed in things are (or be taken to be) qualities belonging by natural right to those things themselves; and hence whatever characteristics we think ourselves able to discern in the universe as a whole are (or be taken to be) the underivative characteristics of the universe itself'.[6] This principle is in effect a rather more comprehensive version of the principle of natural explanation. Whereas the latter is relevant to natural theology in that it militates against positing divine intervention *in* the cosmos as the explanation of various puzzles, the former militates too against positing divine action *on* the cosmos such as features in cosmological and cosmic teleological arguments.

Yet appeal to the Stratonician principle does not clinch the issue against the proponent of the argument from contingency. For, firstly, one of the characteristics which some people think themselves able to discern in the universe as a whole is . . . contingency, that is to say, a characteristic which presents intellectual problems apparently soluble only by appeal to an ontologically self-sufficient transcendent being; and this characteristic is indeed regarded as belonging by natural right to the cosmos, in the sense that the cosmos considered in itself, independently of any putative transcendent being, is judged to be ontologically insecure. Thus if appeal is made to the Stratonician principle (together with Occam's razor) against the principle of sufficient reason by pointing out that the cosmos does continue, and hence should be regarded as intrinsically capable of continuing, the appeal may be counterbalanced by pointing out that the universe may equally be regarded as intrinsically

capable of ceasing, and that its not having done so is finally satisfactorily intelligible only when it is considered in connection
with the contrasting mode of existence of a CEB. (This point
about intelligibility applies also to the possible suggestion that
one might as well posit an unknown universal immanent 'natural' existence-continuing cause as the ground of the cosmos's
continued existence as posit a transcendent being.) Here the
move is made to (*c*) as also to the second point. For, secondly, it
may be argued that the drive for intelligibility which is being
trusted by those who accept the principle of sufficient reason
would not be being trusted fully if the Stratonician principle,
even in combination with Occam's razor, were allowed precedence over it. Here, however, it is necessary to be clearer
about the status of this drive and the nature of the principle of
sufficient reason as used in the present argument, and this is
considered below.

Nevertheless the significance of the demand for intelligibility
here may briefly be brought out in another way. The shift from
Aristotelian to Newtonian physics involves on the one hand
ceasing to take states of inertia for granted, and on the other
hand beginning to regard as natural and as not requiring explanation such phenomena as the persistent motion of celestial
bodies. Now it is arguable that the proponent of the argument
from contingency is adopting towards the persistent existence
of the world an old-fashioned 'Aristotelian' attitude, which
needs to be replaced by a 'Newtonian' one. Yet it is open to
him to reply that the justification for the switch to the Newtonian view was the overall increased yield in intelligibility,
and that in the contingency case the overall yield is increased
if the Stratonician view is surrendered in favour of a theistic
one. Here again considerations adduced later (in connection
with 'empirical fit') are highly pertinent for assessing the
range of intelligibility.

It remains for us to proceed on the lines of (*c*). The preceding discussion sprang from an examination of the notion of an
explanatory terminus. This notion was found to be acceptable
in the cases of purposive explanation and natural theoretical
explanation. The possibility of a non-natural explanatory terminus, whether theoretical or purposive or of some other
kind, is now explored, being an attempt to chart a middle

course between the unacceptable alternatives of a non-natural explanation of the cosmos in terms of a logically necessary being, and one in terms of an infinite series of non-natural beings.

(ii)

The explanation sought is a non-natural explanation, that is to say, an explanation in terms of something beyond the cosmos. Attention was drawn in Chapter 1 to the problems besetting talk about anything being 'beyond' the cosmos, and an attempt made to relieve the difficulties by indicating the problematic nature of talk about ourselves. In all discourse concerning ourselves as putative non-material subjects there is an irreducible analogical element. 'I' presents us with an inescapable mystery, an elusive entity which must be located '"in" the world' rather than straightforwardly 'in the world'. It is temporally immersed but spacially ambiguous. And this ineradicable analogical character of 'in' as used of it affords us logical licence to use 'in' in an other than straightforward manner of a transcendent being. Conversely, it seems permissible to say that the self is in some sense 'beyond' physical space (or indeed also 'beyond' the mental space occupied or constituted by its images). If then we are to speak of a cosmos-explaining-being or CEB 'beyond' the world or 'in' it, then it is only natural to take the self as a model and conceive of the CEB as a cosmic self (or cosmic 'self', for it will differ from human selves in vital respects). This model is in any case in our minds because of the context of the discussion, but it should be stressed that in point of logic there is a path to the model which is dependent not on religion but on purely philosophical considerations.

It is suggested therefore that the spirituality of the CEB be introduced speculatively near the beginning of the argument rather than putatively deductively near the end as in Owen's. 'Spirituality' rather than 'non-materiality' strictly speaking, if indeed the two be not equivalent, because spirituality is the only kind of non-materiality which we know in connection with beings, and non-materiality as distinct from spirituality could not function in an *explanatory* hypothesis. In what follows, however, the terms are not in fact distinguished.

Before proceeding I must make clear how the word 'self' is

being used here. It is arguable, as already indicated, that the mental events constituting the mind need to be distinguished from the physical events constituting the brain. It is further arguable that mental events need to be distinguished from a non-material subject of those events. Thus, for example, if we take the case of awareness of a mental image, analysis of this act of awareness reveals, on this view, that in addition to the mental image we need to speak of a non-material perceiver of the image. This non-material perceiver or subject is the 'self'. Alternatively, 'self' is 'I', the ultimate elusive subject of one's own experience.

There is no space to debate this point at length, any more than it is possible to debate the mind–brain identity issue. I wish now simply to presuppose mind–brain dualism; but let me ground my view of the self briefly in an appeal to each person's experience of being a subject of experiences and not simply the experiences themselves, of being the beholder of mental images rather than the images themselves. The appeal is finally to introspection and self-analysis. Not that the self is patient of observation (as is a mental image) or description (as is a thought or feeling), and to suppose that it is is to bark with Hume up the wrong tree. Yet it is most certainly, in my view, patient of apprehension, as profound reflection by any individual on what he finally means by 'I' should reveal. The argument of Chapter 8 (or more particularly of the article to which I there refer) provides further support for this view, with regard especially to its intelligibility, and provided this intelligibility is allowed, the main burden of my argument should stand.

Returning now to the argument, further progress may be made by inquiring into the possible nature of the relationship between the putative CEB and the cosmos. If such relationship there be, then from our point of view it is clearly one of dependence. Yet there are many kinds of dependence: the dependence of baby on adult, of whole on part or part on whole, of present on past, and so on. Nevertheless, we have the important datum that the dependence in question is one of dependence on a self. Moreover, since what calls for explanation is the character of the ongoing existence of every part of the cosmos, the dependence of the cosmos on this self will be total. What needs to be asked therefore is whether there is anything

in any individual's experience which is totally dependent on
his activity as a non-material subject.

There may appear not to be, for all experience is conditioned
by the world and/or by past experience. Yet in a sense there is
an aspect of every person's experience which is totally dependent on his subjective activity. The world would not appear to
him as it does did he not see it as he does, and his seeing it as he
does is due to his powers of organising incoming data. The process of experiencing is a process of interpretation and reinterpretation. And what are these? Surely a creative going beyond
the immediate evidence. This is vividly illustrated of course in
cases of seeing-as. Consider the goblet/faces puzzle picture. I
see it now as one thing, now as another. What happens between? A 'creative switch' would surely be an apt description. If
then we seek a model in subjective activity by which to interpret
a putative cosmological relation of dependence, human creativity suggests itself forcibly. Is the adoption of such a model
fruitful? For fruitfulness is after all the prime requirement in
any explanatory hypothesis.

It is necessary first, however, to be rather clearer as to what is
involved in creativity at the human level. It has been claimed
that experiencing is a creative going beyond the immediate evidence. This is at once intelligible as standing in opposition to
the old-fashioned empiricist view according to which experience and knowledge are the result of sense-impressions im-
pressing themselves on passive recipients. But what more
precisely is involved?

To urge that experiencing involves personal activity rather
than passivity is to urge that there is action originating in the
self and not merely originated by the action on the self of external stimuli. Thus the sufficiency of the world's action on us for
experience of that world is denied. I have just urged that in addition to the mental event which is a thought or feeling, we need
the thinker or feeler. The idea of action originating in the self
connects with this idea of the thinker or feeler. At a given
instant in the life of a person there is both interpretation and in-
terpreter, both a seeing and a seer. The self is an autonomous
centre of outgoing, structuring activity as well as the partial
product of incoming forces. (Indeed, taking 'centre' here seriously, a suggestion for a terse definition of 'self' might be 'A

subject-point-instant located "in" the world'.)

The notion of action originating in the self connects too with the problem of free-will. If we say that at a given instant the action of a person really does *originate* in the self at that instant, in part at least, then although it is crucially conditioned by previous experience, habit, training and so on, it is not totally determined by antecedent causes, whether mental or physical. Free-will may thus be seen as the capacity for conditioned spontaneity – the capacity for origination within a context.

Now if account is taken of the active interpretative nature of all experiencing, on this view there is an element of freedom in all experiencing, though frequently minimal or apparently subordinate. It is the background of all mental activity (unless qualifications need be introduced in cases such as developed mystical experience, certain kinds of hypnotic trance, or control of the mind by drugs). To suggest this is not of course to deny that there is a dense ordering of physical and mental *causes* and effects. It is to deny that such a continuum is the whole story. To each mental event there needs to be added not only its causal relations to prior and to succeeding events and to its subject self, but also a dimension of freedom, a dimension of 'originating in the self'. There is no strict determination of mental events by prior causes, whether mental or physical, though very often for all practical purposes such determination may be assumed. Moreover, not only is the action originating in the self not totally explicable in terms of the action of mental or physical causes, but also the action originating in the 'self-now' is not entirely explicable in terms of the effect on the 'self-now' of the 'self-as-it-was'. It is, in fact, *original*.

The problem of free-will is frequently discussed in connection with moments of grave moral decision or the question of creative genius. This is perfectly legitimate, for in such cases the issues present themselves most forcibly. For example, however difficult it may be to find a viable conception of free-will as an alternative to determinism on the one hand or random lack of causation on the other, if the reality and significance of moral choice are not to be repudiated, the attempt to find a viable alternative must be continued.[7] It can be misleading, however, to confine discussion to these particular cases, for the scope of the problem tends to be distorted. There are thus advantages in broaching it in a broader context.

Incidentally it is an error, and a methodological error, to take the difficulty of conceiving personal freedom as a viable alternative to either determinism or randomness to be an insuperable obstacle to talking of personal freedom at all. For in the final analysis the problem of freedom, of creativity, of personal activity in the experiencing process, is the problem of what occurs mentally in any instant which is the physical present for a particular person; and of this we can be quite sure, that what must elude precise conceptualisation and linguistic definition is the nature of mental activity occurring in the physical present. For the physical present is instantaneous, but conscious experience is always in 'drops'. Thus the path of mental activity through a series of instants can be traced, but it cannot be tracked down as it occurs at each instant. Again, the problem of freedom and personal creativity is the problem of that personal subjectivity which necessarily defies objectification. It concerns the mystery of 'I-now'. We can only murmur 'origination', 'creation', 'conditioned spontaneity', in an attempt to grasp, and to convey by getting others to grasp, an element in our individual experience which is unique in character and which must be experienced to be known.

The preceding analysis gives some account then of the model which suggests itself as a means of interpreting a putative cosmological relation of dependence. Again, it must be insisted that although this model of creativity is in any case in our minds because of the theistic context of the discussion, the considerations adduced are valid independent grounds for choosing it.

The question of fruitfulness may now opportunely be taken up. If the model is to prove its worth there are three necessary conditions to be fulfilled. It must (a) provide an *explanation* of the world's continuing to be; (b) provide a *non-natural* explanation; and (c) provide a non-natural explanatory *terminus*.

The first condition is easily met if we suppose that the world is dependent on a transcendent creative subject ('transcendent' here meaning 'not part of the cosmos'). For example, there is a sense in which a creative musician sustains a new composition 'in his head' before ever pen is put to paper or finger to keyboard, and it is possible to see here an illuminating analogy for a possible creative, sustaining action of a CEB on the world.

Again, the creation of the world is traditionally held to be creation 'out of nothing'. Now when a composer produces a new symphony or whatever, there enters into the world something completely novel and, if the remarks above on freedom have any validity, unpredictable, dependent indeed on the composer's previous knowledge and experience but not totally explicable in terms of them. In a very real sense, therefore, they are 'out of nothing': original – *ex nihilo*.

Yet again, the interpretation of ontological dependence in terms of dependence upon a personal creativity chimes in fruitfully with that sense of contingency which forms the basis of the present discussion. The consideration that for all the world teaches us otherwise it could simply cease to exist and could have ceased to exist at any time, resembles strikingly, for example, considerations which may arise from attending to someone speaking, namely that for aught we can tell from attending to the words alone the voice might simply desist, and might have done so at any time. All depends on the will of the creative utterer (and most speech is creation, to however limited an extent). All depends on the will of the creator.

Thus far then the analogy is fruitful. A putative transcendent creative subject would appear able to meet the first condition by providing an ontological foundation for the cosmos, thereby explaining its continuance and explaining it in a way that fits well our experience of contingency. Admittedly, we have no clear understanding of the nature of transcendent sustaining creativity, but then the same applies to human creativity; and the latter furnishes models which are sufficiently illuminating to warrant our claiming that it is intelligible to say *that* there may be transcendent sustaining creativity even though we cannot say *how* such activity operates.

With regard to the second condition, although the human subject is non-material it is clearly natural or a part of nature (such at any rate is the assumption here, based partly on acceptance of the principle of natural explanation), and an explanation in terms of human creativity is a natural explanation. In what sense would explanation in terms of a creative CEB be non-natural? Quite simply in the sense that it would be redundant as a natural explanation. Although the putative CEB is modelled on personal creativity, his creativity is not part of the world as is human creativity. Thus to the model there needs to be added, in I. T. Ramsey's term, a 'qualifier'. Whereas human creativity is essentially related (in this world) to human bodies and to a conditioning network of physical causes, the creativity of the CEB is not. We may perhaps say that it is related to a body, that the cosmos is its body, but that should serve only to emphasise the *difference* between the creativity of the CEB and human creativity and between their respective relations to the world. Human creativity is dependent on its body; the body of the CEB is dependent on his creativity.

It follows of course that the CEB is not 'in' (or 'beyond') the world in precisely the way that human selves may be said to be 'in' it. Otherwise he would be part of it. This difference does not, however, ruin the propriety of taking the self as a model for a CEB. In talk about a CEB there must be an irreducible spatial analogy. If the former is valid, why should not the latter be? And why not take the former as a clue to the latter? Indeed, we have begun to see such a procedure paying dividends.

A creative CEB modelled on the creative human self thus appears capable of meeting the second condition also, that of supplying a *non-natural* explanation of the cosmos. If we are to have a CEB at all, the notion developed so far appears to be on the right lines. Already we have the basis of a more illuminating and consistent hypothesis than Owen's, albeit one reached in a rather 'looser' way than his attempts at deducing the conclusion strictly from given premises. The approach is 'soft' rather than 'hard'.

What of the third condition? For we have yet to see how the postulation of such a being can be prevented from leading to a vicious infinite regress. Why does a CEB not necessitate a CEBEB, which necessitates a CEBEBEB, and so on?

The argument being developed draws much inspiration from N. Smart's discussion in *Philosophers and Religious Truth*. Now when Smart considers the objection that the CEB might itself be in need of further explanation, he replies: 'What we must remember is that the object of an explanation is to produce a gain in intelligibility. To postulate a further Being beyond the CEB will not, I suspect, help in this direction.' Munitz too reaches this conclusion: 'Whether or not it, in turn, led to the posing of further questions about itself, would not in any way diminish the effectiveness of the answer such a reason-for-the-existence-of-the-world would give to the mystery of the existence of the world.' Flew on the other hand refers in this connection to Smart's 'seemingly arbitrary proceedings, and not proceedings'; and while disagreement was registered earlier with his charge that 'it is to satisfy a demand for explanation in distinctly personal terms that the take-off is made into a scientifically redundant dimension', it is difficult not to sympathise when he continues, 'and it is, presumably, because the accommodation required can be provided there that the journey ends at the first stop'.[8]

The difficulty with the Smart – Munitz position is that it fails to do justice to the quest for a *final* explanation. Perhaps, says Smart, we can 'simply content ourselves with speaking of a CEB, without delving into the mysteries of what (if anything) lies beyond. Entities are not to be multiplied beyond necessity.'[9] In terms of an earlier part of the present discussion this is tantamount to saying that we should separate the two functions of the Janus-questions and restrict ourselves to one. But as pointed out then, the two functions are closely related. Is there a real gain in intelligibility if the postulated CEB is as contingent as that which it is invoked to explain? Is it not rather the case that the problem remains unresolved but its scope widened? It is all very well to develop, as Smart suggests, a richer notion of a CEB than is contained in the notion 'cosmos-explaining-being' alone. Nevertheless the deeper questions remain and are not squarely faced. Is his CEB ultimate or not? If it is, why is it? Because a CEBEB would not be a gain in intelligibility? But if a CEB is a gain in intelligibility, why would a CEBEB not be? On the other hand, if his CEB is not ultimate, if the prospect is an infinite regress, few will feel justified in launching out on an argument from contingency. Occam's razor will and should be wielded from the start. For whereas the extension of the temporal causal regress to infinity is a hypothesis which is both in line with our knowledge of causal sequences within limited time-spans and also does not leave a surd of unintelligibility with regard to causality (though it does with regard to ontological continuance), the postulation of an infinity of Explanatory Beings is neither the prolongation of a known limited series of such Beings, nor a satisfactory solution to the problem of ontological continuance, since the problem recurs with regard to each allegedly Explanatory Being.

In his *Arguments for the Existence of God*, Hick contends that because we are ourselves conscious beings 'we can accept the existence of purposive intelligence as an ultimate fact, neither requiring nor permitting explanation in terms of anything more ultimate than itself'. Such acceptance of a transcendent intelligence as the self-explanatory explanation of the cosmos is not a demonstration of his existence, but it is not in the least irrational, says Hick. Yet in the present context such a view is quite unacceptable. The puzzle giving rise to the quest for explanation concerns ontological continuance. Nothing in Hick's account suggests that this puzzle would not occur equally in connection with the existence of a transcendent purposive intelligence. Moreover, quite apart from this context his thesis is unacceptable. He urges 'the general priority of mind over matter, from the point of view of mind, in the explanatory hierarchy'. Thus he grades purposive explanation above causal (and theoretical) explanation. (A similar bias in favour of purposive explanation constitutes the core of G. F. Woods's otherwise helpful *Theological Explanation*.) Yet there is simply no ground for such grading. A purposive explanation of why Whillans and Haston climbed Annapurna South Face is no better as an explanation than a causal or theoretical explanation of why iceblocks collapsed killing their expedition companion, Clough. In this sense there is no explanatory hierarchy.[10]

Yet it so happens that the notion of a CEB sketched so far lends itself extraordinarily, indeed apparently uniquely, well to being developed as a non-natural explanatory ultimate. This must now be indicated, drawing on recent discussions of divine necessity.

The key term in the notion of a CEB hitherto is creativity, and here lies the key also to that further development which forms the final justification for adhering to the model. It has been noted that the creativity of the CEB differs from human creativity in that it does not operate within narrow limits. The world is created out of nothing. What is now suggested is that the notion of sheer creativity be taken totally seriously, and the CEB be conceived as creating not only the world but itself too.

That this is properly conceivable may be brought out by reference to process thought, for in a modified process theism is to be found an invaluable model for a developed CEB.

In Whitehead's system God is a single actual entity, but as developed by Hartshorne and J. Cobb he becomes a personal series of actual entities each of which creates its successor. Now whatever the defects of this atomistic approach, the series' ability to sustain itself does not appear to be open to serious question. But if not, then neither would it be open to question in the case of a personal series composed of durationless experient-occasions. Yet such a series could be regarded as a self-creating continuant, each durationless 'temporal part' of which creates both its creative successor and the world. Such a concept of self-creation is awe-inspiring, but it seems to be perfectly intelligible and capable of playing an integral role in the developed concept of a CEB. (I have modified process theism, changing the CEB into a changing continuant, partly, though this is not the place to argue the point, because I regard the process view(s) as incoherent, and partly because outside process thought the self or human subject is generally, and in my view rightly, regarded as a changing continuant.)

The doctrine of the continuous re-creation of the world at each successive instant is found in Descartes, and as such evokes from F. R. Tennant the criticism that it is a 'fancy . . . as baseless and as non-explanatory as it is inconsistent with either theism or fact-controlled metaphysics. It implies that there are no souls or substances, no causes but God, no meaning in the world save for its Creator.'[11] However, the whole point of introducing durationless experient-occasions is ultimately precisely to justify belief in 'souls or substances'; and the charge that the notion of re-creation does away with all causes except God (or rather, at this stage of the argument, except the CEB) may only be sustained if creation and causation are equated with each other. Clearly, however, the two must be distinguished, for otherwise creation cannot serve the purpose for which it was introduced, namely to operate as an explanation of the contingency involved in the causal nexus. Yet if it is distinguished from causation, or said to be a different mode of causation, it is possible to suppose that the CEB's creation of the world at each instant is creation of the world *as caused by its predecessors*. Then if the synoptic view is taken, the picture is of a creative continuant sustaining 'substance-causes' (Tennant) or the causal nexus. Or, we might say, the CEB provides the sustaining dimension within which the causal dimension rests. He is the condition of causality, or its ontological presupposition.

Now since the cosmos is a causal nexus it may be said to be autonomous. But since the causal nexus is dependent on a transcendent sustaining power, the autonomy is limited or delegated. Yet not in such a way as to deny that it may be a source of meaning for others than its Creator. And it is possible to agree with a further thesis of Tennant's that 'theism must be sufficiently tinged with deism to recognise a settled order, and an order in which the causation is not immediate divine causation', a thesis which is essential if there is to be any prospect of seriously coping with the problems of suffering and evil.[12] There is thus no genuine incompatibility between Tennant's basic position and the position adopted here.

Still another way of expressing the point about the delegated autonomy of the world is to say that God's, or rather the CEB's, creation-sustaining activity is a necessary but not a sufficient condition of intra-cosmic events. This, however, invites the resurgence of a criticism encountered earlier. The implication of the above thesis is that intra-cosmic action is a necessary condition of intra-cosmic events. Yet if it is a necessary condition of such events, then, it might be urged, they cannot require a transcendent explanation for they have a natural one, namely that – causality – by virtue of which the action of a putative transcendent sustainer would not be a sufficient condition of intra-cosmic events.

This objection would be powerful provided that one were justified in collapsing the distinction between the act of existing and the act of causing. Yet it is vastly plausible to take the logical distinction between the two as a reflection of an ontological distinction – thus it is intelligible to speak of a timeless noncausal existent; and when this is done the objection remains innocuous. For the experience of contingency may still be interpreted as an awareness of the ontological frailty of the cosmos's continuing existence; while unease at so interpreting the experience may be taken as deriving from an awareness of the self-sufficiency of intra-cosmic causal activity *qua* causal, and thus of the limited independence of the cosmos. Acceptance of causal action as a necessary condition of intra-cosmic events does not entail its sufficiency as a condition.

To return then to Tennant, it is arguable indeed that the position outlined above fits his needs better than does his own. In place of continuous re-creation or ontological maintenance he has a deity 'sustaining the order of the world as a whole by "rapport" with, or action upon, its more or less perduring constituent elements'. Yet earlier he argues that cosmic teleology involves a Creator as well as a Designer; that creation involves a 'planting out' of things as '*onta*' other than the Creator; and that although this notion of 'planting out' or 'positing' is inexplicable, it should not be conceived as a single event in time 'confined to decreeing the world's primary collocations'. But if it is not so confined presumably it is continuous; and despite the alleged inexplicability of 'planting out', it is clearly more than a continuous ordering of already existent entities. What remains if not continuous re-creation or ontological maintenance? Tennant incidentally takes these to be different, but here they are taken to be two ways of saying the same thing. For if creation did not occur at a single time, yet the doctrine of creation is accepted, what could the difference amount to?[13]

(A further criticism of Tennant's is that 'it seems superfluous to suppose that the beings which God creates or plants out, with existence-for-self, needs must be evanescent according to their own natures, as if createdness implied fleetingness, and that they can only be rendered perduring by continuous new outputs of divine creativity'. This no doubt explains to a very large extent his preference for cosmic teleology and virtual neglect of the argument from contingency.[14] However, the present argument is not based on a mere supposition but on the evaluation of a significant type of experience, and in view of the numerous considerations adduced in this evaluation, Tennant's dismissal of the topic must seem disappointing.)

It should be added that the distinction drawn between causality and creativity has seemed to some a grave flaw in any argument from contingency. The argument gains momentum, it is alleged, from consideration of the fact that every event has a cause, but loses it as soon as it is said that God (or a CEB) is not a cause in this sense. However, as presented here the argument has a broader basis, gaining momentum from consideration of the nature of the ongoing active existence of the causal nexus and from the principle of sufficient reason, of which the causal principle to which appeal is being made in the objection is a more restricted version. The difference between the alleged 'cosmological relation' and causality seems in this context acceptable, and the argument so far able to avoid what to Flew has seemed a Scylla and Charybdis of such arguments, namely that 'in so far as causal explanation is interpreted ordinarily, the "vertical dimension" [involving a 'cosmological relation'] appears to be superfluous; while to the extent that some more exotic construction is provided, the quest for causes in this new sense cannot legitimately inherit the compulsiveness of the more workaday kind of inquiry'.[15]

That the nature of the cosmological relation remains mysterious is no real problem either, despite what is sometimes claimed. 'Everything that is not reducible to other things must be apprehended itself for what it is. Thus there can be no question of defining such a relation.' Any attempt to do so 'declares simply what difference it makes (existence/non-existence) and to what it makes it (the finite inclusively considered)'.[16] It may nevertheless perhaps be illuminated metaphorically, as when it is said that whereas causation operates horizontally, creation operates vertically.

Thus the notion of a self-and-world-creating continuant appears able to survive these criticisms. Let us therefore pursue its implications.

The characterisation of the CEB as self-creating amounts to saying that it is ontologically self-sufficient. Now what after all does it really mean to say this? It means that no other being is needed in order to account for the continuing existence of the putative CEB; that it is ontologically independent; that its existence (tensed), unlike that of the world, gives no grounds for puzzlement and no sign of calling for explanation. Consequently it is a satisfactory candidate for explanatory ultimacy.

The point may be made in a different way. The CEB is invoked to clear up the puzzle of the ontological continuance of the world. From one point of view, we saw, this puzzle may be seen as involving dissatisfaction with the causal type of explanation. If we ask 'Why does the world exist now?' and are given an answer in terms of the causal efficacy of the world in a previous state (or in previous states), the answer is felt to be incomplete. A comparable question asked of the CEB, however, 'Why does the CEB exist now?', may be given a comparable answer which is not felt to be incomplete. For the present existence of the CEB is accountable for in terms of previous activity of the CEB. Whereas the cosmos has no control over its continuing, the CEB does.

It follows that Flew is mistaken when he writes that 'the deficiency required by the Argument from Contingency is not in fact a remediable insufficiency in things'.[17] Whitehead says of God and the world that 'both are in the grip of the ultimate metaphysical ground, the creative advance into novelty'.[18] Now the world gives every sign of being in such a grip. If that is the last word, however, we have no real ground for affirming the existence of God – or rather, here, a CEB. If on the other hand we ask the question which Whitehead apparently does not take seriously, 'Why is it that a world exists?', then on a tensed interpretation of the question we do have a reason for affirming the existence of a CEB, provided that, far from being in the grip of creative advance, it does its own gripping.

(One reason for Whitehead's not taking world-contingency questions seriously is to be found in his remark. 'It belongs to the essence of the universe, that it passes into a future.'[19] The context of this comment is an apologia for a physics in which process is essential, and a critique of the Newtonian account of velocity and momentum. Yet the conclusion that passage into the future belongs to the very essence of the cosmos simply does not follow from any dissatisfaction with the formulation of scientific laws, such as those concerning velocity and momentum for example. For the laws describe the way in which the universe does work and will work if it continues to work in the same way; they do not prescribe that it must so work, that they must continue to apply, that that to which they apply must continue to be, or even that there should continue to be anything to which any laws apply.)

If the answer in terms of the CEB's previous activity is to be ultimately satisfying, however, it is necessary to suppose that the CEB is without beginning. For otherwise it would be necessary to suppose either that the CEB was caused to be by another being, or just happened into existence. The latter is conceivable but profoundly dissatisfying – 'nothing comes from nothing'; the former either leads to an infinity of beings and thus a vicious regress, or ends in a more ultimate CEB of infinite duration, in which case beings have been multiplied beyond necessity.

An infinity of beings is a vicious regress because there is then no explanatory terminus. The temporal infinity of a CEB is not vicious because it occurs as part of an explanatory terminus. That this is so must be shown in greater detail. Here the problem of the tenseless questions (2), (4) and (6) is taken up, as also that of corresponding questions concerning a CEB.

The upshot of the remarks about ontological self-sufficiency is that the question 'Why is there a CEB?' (tensed 'is') is a silly question. It is sometimes said that to explain something is to assign a cause to it or to place it in a wider context where it no longer puzzles us. As the concept is developed above, the CEB is self-caused and hence calls for no other cause; and as the creator of all (else) that is, it stands in no wider context – on the contrary, its creative action constitutes the context in which all else stands. The CEB is thus far acceptable as an ultimate *explicans*, one which itself calls for no further explanation.

But if 'Why is there a CEB?' (tensed 'is') is silly, what of its tenseless counterpart, 'Why is there a CEB?' (tenseless 'is')? Is that a silly question? If so, why? And what about questions (2), (4) and (6) – which for the purposes of the present argument may all be treated as equivalent?

It is necessary at this point to endorse whole-heartedly a contention frequently held to be fatal to arguments from contingency. It is expressed with characteristic vigour by Flew:

At every stage explanation is in terms of something else which, at that stage, has to be accepted as a brute fact. In some further stage that fact itself may be explained; but still in terms of something else which, at least temporarily, has simply to be accepted. . . . It would therefore seem to be a consequence of the essential nature of explanation that, however much may ultimately be explained in successive stages of inquiry, there must always be some facts which have simply to be accepted with what Samuel Alexander used to call 'natural piety'. . . . [And this is] not a contingent fact about one sort of system, but a logical truth about all explanations of facts. The ultimate facts about God would have to be, for precisely the same reason, equally inexplicable. In each and every case we must necessarily find at the end of every explanatory road some ultimates which have simply to be accepted as the fundamental truths about the way things are. And this itself is a contention, not about the lamentable contingent facts of the human condition, but about what follows necessarily from the nature of explanation.[20]

It is impossible to see how any of this can be denied once the notion of logically necessary existence is renounced.

If that be so, however, the final explanatory power of the CEB may be expressed thus. That the transcendent creative self is (tenseless 'is') is no more self-explanatory than that the world (or the causal nexus) is (tenseless 'is'). But that the transcendent creative self is (tensed 'is') *is* more self-explanatory than that the world is (tensed 'is').

The justification of the second of these claims has already been offered. The first calls for further comment. In what sense, it may be asked, is the CEB an explanatory terminus if the fact that it is (tenseless 'is') is no more self-explanatory than that the cosmos is (tenseless 'is')?

The answer is that in view of the endorsement of Flew's contention it may as well be said that the fact that the CEB is (tenseless 'is') is not, strictly, self-explanatory at all; it is something to be accepted with 'natural piety'. For it is arguable in this connection that, in general, the fact that x is (tenseless 'is') can never in itself be a proper cause for puzzlement, whatever the value of x. It can only be a proper cause for puzzlement if the understanding of what x is (tensed 'is') is puzzling. Certainly this holds where x is either the world or a CEB. For if the existence (tenseless) of the world may legitimately be questioned in its own right, then so may that of a CEB, which means that a CEBEB should be introduced, the existence (tenseless) of which could also legitimately be questioned, and so on in a vicious infinite regress. The only way of avoiding this is to apply Occam's razor to the CEB and see in the fact that the world exists (tenseless) nothing that genuinely calls for further explanation.

In the case of the world, however, the view advocated here is that our understanding of its existing (tensed) is genuinely puzzling. Therefore, provided that it is interpreted in the light of this puzzle, 'Why is it that the world exists?' (tenseless), as also questions (4) and (6), may legitimately be asked. The question would then read, 'Why is it that the *world* exists?' (tenseless). Apart from this context, however, the tenseless world-contingency questions are silly. In a phrase used earlier, they are 'not fully rational', for they attempt to press 'why' beyond the limits which circumscribe the area of its profitable and therefore proper usage.

In the case of the CEB, by contrast, our understanding of its existing (tensed) is not genuinely puzzling. That the CEB is (tenseless 'is') may be for us a source of wonder, as indeed in a sense it may be for him, but neither in us nor in him can his continuing to exist occasion perplexity or intellectual dissatisfaction, and neither therefore can the fact that he exists (tenseless 'exists'). Similarly, the silliness of 'Why is it that a CEB exists?' (tenseless 'exists') follows from the impropriety of 'Why is it that a CEB exists?' (tensed 'exists').

The CEB has yet to be identified with God, but it is convenient to make brief mention at this juncture of the following two points, in both of which reference to God might be replaced by reference to a CEB.

Firstly, Owen has replied to Flew's objection that sooner or later we are bound to accept ultimate facts which are inexplicable, and that God is no less inexplicable than the world, by urging that it 'rests on a confusion between two senses of "inexplicable". If the finite world is taken as ultimate it is inexplicable in the sense that its existence *cannot* be explained. If God is taken as ultimate he is inexplicable in the sense that his existence *does not need* to be explained. . . .' Owen here scores a nice point but falls down when justifying it by continuing, '. . . for being One whose essence is identical with existence he is self-explanatory'.[21] The objections to this were mentioned earlier. On the other hand the arguments of the present section constitute a satisfactory justification of his point.

Secondly, A. Plantinga has argued interestingly that the

synthetic proposition 'God exists' shares with analytic propositions such as 'All vacuums are empty' the characteristic
that in connection with it the question 'Why is it that . . .?'
cannot arise. 'Why is it that God exists?' is as absurd as 'Why is
it that all vacuums are empty?' This characteristic is one which
it shares with logically necessary statements alone – from which
it is sometimes but falsely argued that it too is logically necessary.[22]

'God exists' has built into it then a logical veto on the question 'Why is it that God exists?' To ask the question is to betray
misunderstanding of what 'God' means. Now 'The world
exists' on the other hand, we know, has no corresponding ban
built into it. As has been indicated it is possible to develop an
argument to the effect that 'Why is it that the world exists?'
(tenseless 'exists') is on its own a silly question, but that is not a
conclusion that may be drawn purely from an analysis of the
conept 'world' (or 'cosmos').

The significance of this from the point of view of the argument propounded here may now be put very briefly. Just as the
logical contingency of 'The world exists' is a reflection of the
world's factual contingency, so the linguistic impropriety of
'Why is it that God exists?', far from being a mere linguistic
freak, reflects the differing ontological status of the respective
referents. Nevertheless, Plantinga's account is not entirely
accurate from the point of view of the argument of the present
chapter, for he fails to distinguish between tensed and tenseless
versions of 'God exists'. His thesis is sound in connection with
the former; but with regard to the latter, the question 'Why is it
that God exists?' (tenseless 'exists') need not betray misunderstanding of what 'God' means. It may be assigned a certain
formal validity and interpreted as asking why the (tenseless)
logical possibility, nothing (a possibility which follows from the
fact that 'God exists' is not logically necessary), is (tenseless
'is') a possibility and not an actuality. Why is it the case (tenseless 'is') that God is (tenseless 'is') and not nothing? This question is, I have urged, silly or not fully rational, for it disregards
that essential aspect of explanation highlighted by Flew; but it
does not betray misunderstanding of 'God'.

Now here reference may conveniently be made back to that
other group of contingency questions, consideration of which

was deferred in Chapter 2, consisting of, for example, 'Why is there anything at all?', 'Why does anything exist?' If these are taken to mean something approximately equal to 'Why do any of these things around us exist?' (tensed 'exist') then they may be equated with question (1), 'Why is it that the world exists?' If they are taken to mean something approximately equal to 'Why is it that something or other exists?' (tensed 'exists'), where 'something or other' implicitly refers to the kind of thing experienced in the world, then they may be equated with question (3), 'Why is it that a world exists?'

On the other hand they may be taken to mean something approximately equal to 'Why is it that the logical possibility, nothing, is a possibility only and not an actuality?' (tenseless 'is'). In that case, for reasons given already, they are silly questions.

It follows that when advocates of arguments from contingency urge contemplation of the possibility that nothing might exist, what P. Tillich calls 'the shock of non-being', their exhortation needs cautious scrutiny. For if what it amounts to is that 'nothing' is (tenseless 'is') a logically possible alternative to the total situation described by 'The world exists' (tenseless 'exists'), then the exercise of contemplating this possibility cannot yield anything in the way of an argument from contingency. It could do so only if the tenseless world-contingency questions (2), (4) and (6) were sensible in their own right, and we have seen that they are not. What it amounts to is an exhortation to ask 'Why is there anything at all?' interpreted as a 'silly' question.

(Also the falsity (with regard to the kind of deity relevant here) of Tillich's claim that 'even a god would disappear [in the abyss of possible non-being] if he were not being-itself' should now be clear.[23] If there is a CEB (who may be identified as a god) there is no factual possibility of non-being into the abyss of which he may disappear; and although even if a CEB exists there is a (tenseless) logical possibility of non-being which he may envisage, it is certainly not an abyss which he need regard as a threat.)

Yet if what is intended by the exhortation to contemplate nothingness is an exhortation to consider the nature of the ongoing existence of the world and to relate it to an ever-present possibility, even if it is said to be 'only in theory', of its simply ceasing, the exhortation is valid. (A difficulty with N. Smart's argument from contingency is that it is not clear which he is advocating, though from considerations which will be mentioned later it would unfortunately appear to be the former.) For the exercise of contemplating this possibility can engender the question 'Why is there anything at all?' in the sense of questions (1), (3) and (5), questions which far from being silly are profoundly rational, pressing 'why' beyond its everyday limits admittedly, but not beyond its legitimate limits, and penetrating intellectual depths unsuspected in the straightforward pursuit of everyday practical or scientific theoretical aims – or many philosophical ones.

Thus, to return for a moment to the very beginning of Chapter 2, the experience of contingency which is able, if anything is, to form a sound basis for an argument from contingency must be an experience which finds its proper expression, not in world-contingency questions of the silly variety such as (2), (4) and (6) taken in isolation, but in their verbally identical counterparts, questions (1), (3) and (5). And in fact contingency$_5$ may now be restricted to that experience which relates to tensed world-contingency questions, and the experience which relates to tenseless world-contingency questions labelled experience of contingency$_6$. It would then appear that Wittgenstein's remarks relate strongly to an experience of contingency$_6$ rather than contingency$_5$. Yet it may well involve the latter also, the two failing to be distinguished as perhaps frequently in discussions of arguments from contingency, and it may thus in its ambiguity legitimately be taken as a starting-point for the present analysis.

Yet 'finds its proper expression . . . in' is a one-sided way of viewing the matter. Equally one might say 'is engendered by'. For although the questions may arise from a certain emotional or contemplative mood, equally such a mood may be occasioned by the questions, as expressed perhaps by someone else. In that case the mood is a product of rational reflection rather than, as Nielsen would have us believe, an emotional hangover from childhood religious indoctrination; and the rationality of the questions affords some warrant for supposing the mood to be a mode of awareness.

Finally in this connection the distinction between acceptable and unacceptable interpretations of verbally identical questions may throw new light on the recurring disputes between protagonists of arguments from contingency and its opponents. For it may be that the latter have been working with the silly interpretations in mind and the former with the sensible ones, the inevitable talking at cross-purposes contained in their discussions remaining undetected because their opposing views have at crucial points found identical linguistic expression. Neither side has felt compelled to abandon its basic position for the simple reason that, despite the logical acuity of the respective opponents and their ability to destroy various arguments on either side, the rock-bottom bases of their several attacks remain untouched because not precisely formulated and therefore never properly revealed as prime targets. It is at any rate a possibility perhaps worth considering. It would follow of course that the silly interpretations of world-contingency questions are not in fact the ones which most accurately express the experience of contingency which has been a nerve in previous attempts to defend an argument from contingency.

The conclusion which emerges from the foregoing is that the concept of a CEB developed above is indeed able to meet the third condition which it is required to meet, that of providing a non-natural explanatory *terminus*. Consequently at this point such a being must be reckoned to lay serious claim to the credence of any person for whom the continued existence of the world is in any way a problem and not to be taken for granted. What more remains to be said?

The argument has proceeded on the assumption that the principle of sufficient reason is to be accepted, and this remains to be queried. First, however, there is a further aspect of the notion of the CEB as an explanatory terminus which needs to be considered, and it arises from the fact that the CEB is conceived in terms of an active self. For since the *explanans* is personal, questions of purposive explanation arise.

Since they arise only at this stage, however, it is apparent that the present argument is no undignified flight to the personal such as may legitimately be castigated by critics of cosmological arguments. Yet if it is not, in the first instance at least, purposive, is it theoretical? It may be regarded as such, but again not in the first instance. It is so regarded for example if (assuming temporarily that the CEB may be identified with God) one speaks of a basic theistic law such as that suggested by Martin: 'All things happen and are sustained by God's will.'[24] In the first instance, however, the appeal to the CEB is neither theoretical nor purposive – nor of course is it causal. Rather is it 'causal'. The kind of causation involved is not natural historical causation, but transcendent 'creation-causation'. Although it is not straightforwardly causal in the natural intra-mundane sense, however, it clearly belongs to the same 'family' and thus may be labelled 'causal' (' "causal" '). Incidentally it is assumed here that natural historical causality is a matter, not merely of Humean regular sequential occurrence, but of genuine efficacy – a view defended, briefly but cogently, by Owen.[25] Acceptance of such a view facilitates acceptance of the creation-causation view.

Now, however, questions of purposive explanation do indeed arise. Reference has been made so far to a self-creating creative subject without any discussion of whether such a being would or would not be conscious. Now as far as our experience of the contents of the cosmos goes, creativity is at its most highly developed in conscious human endeavour. There would therefore be an air of perversity about regarding the creator of the *cosmos* as less than conscious. It would appear both eminently natural and sensible to suppose rather that the miracle of a self-creating CEB is more rather than less conscious than we; that, if anything, pure creativity is complete consciousness, and the CEB the supreme self. It may or may not be self-contradictory to conceive of the supreme creative self as non-conscious, but the notion is a peculiar one in the light of what we know, and by what other light are we to judge? Once again the reasons given are 'soft' rather than 'hard', but they are reasons none the less.

If, however, the analogy between human personality and the CEB is as close as this, then it may be seen to be fruitful indeed. Consider again the question 'Why is there a CEB?' (tensed 'is'). Suppose it is given a temporal causal-type answer (or temporal 'causal'-type answer). One may then ask: But why does the CEB continue creating itself and the world? Why does it not 'create nothing' by simply refusing to create itself? Why does it not commit suicide?

Well, why do we not commit suicide? On the whole because we value living; and we value living because we value loving and being loved, because we value the beauty of culture and the beauty of nature. Can there be anyone to whom none of these apply? In man at least the will to live is an affirmation of value.

What happens if we suppose the same to be true of the CEB? We find that we have a complete explanation of his continuing to create himself. For if the world is good and if he is good then there is every reason to continue both; and the reason is ultimate – because to continue them is good. 'Why continue what is good?' is, other things being equal, a peculiar or 'silly' question. If an explanation culminates in an affirmation of purpose grounded in and aiming at value, then of its type that explanation is complete and intellectually satisfying. There is neither a going beyond it nor a felt need to go beyond it.

But are other things equal in this case? What of the problems of suffering and of evil? Granted that an explanation in terms of goodness would be satisfactory in theory, can it be countenanced in fact?

It is impossible to pursue these matters here. Suffice it to say that the acceptability of the argument from contingency as developed here is conditional upon the solubility of these twin problems. The assumption is indeed that they are not insuperable, or that there is sufficient reason to suppose them soluble in principle (even in the context of a perfect CEB, see below). Reference may be made to Tennant's excellent treatment of the topic.[26]

It is perhaps conceivable that the CEB might be wicked; that his values be not ours; that ultimately we are the playthings of a despot. Yet such a view seems curious. Would such a being have granted us such a world and the possibility of so much happiness? For despite the suffering and evil most men have a pro-attitude towards the world, an attitude which leads naturally to and would seem to justify a pro-attitude towards a putative creator.

Perhaps it will be objected (with quotation from Hume) that such a view involves an invalid move from the character of the cosmos to that of its creator; for there is only one cosmos and one putative creator whereas for a valid inductive inference several would be needed. This argument is at best a sound rebuttal of the contention that a creator would *probably* be good; but not of the contention that the goodness of the creator seems *plausible*. It would be sound in this regard only if the CEB were 'wholly other' so that analogical inference based on experience of ourselves as creators and valuers were ruled out completely. Yet the notion developed here is not of a wholly other being – such a concept would not indeed make sense. It therefore seems permissible to judge that a putative creator of the world would be worthy of a pro-attitude towards him at least as much as is the world itself. Such a judgement involves perhaps a 'soft' ana- logical inference rather than a relatively 'hard' inductive one, yet when what is being judged is the relation between the world as a whole and a putative *transcendens*, such reasoning is in order.

There are good grounds then for supposing the CEB to be good ('good' in a sense explicitly analogous to that applicable to us), and in his goodness and that of the world we find a satis- factory explanation of his and its continuance. As a non-natural explanatory terminus, therefore, he appears to be acceptable in every respect. Is there indeed a rival? There is nothing in the concept of a necessary being alone, for example, which explains the existence of the cosmos, and as Mascall remarks: 'We may indeed find it strange that there should be such a thing as self- existent being, though if our capacity for wonder is functioning properly we shall see that what is really strange is that there should be anything else.'[27]

It may perhaps be emphasised yet again at this point that the hypothetical postulation of the kind of CEB which has been dis- cussed cannot be dismissed as the product of a yen for anthro- pomorphic satisfaction. The CEB was modelled on the creative self in the first instance because that seemed the natural way of achieving a non-natural explanation. Can any other be suggested? More importantly, however, when the model was developed it was seen to be singularly fruitful. Is any other that may be thought of equally fruitful? If this quest for final theor- etical satisfaction culminates in an explanation in personal terms, then it is only because such an explanation is intel- lectually satisfactory.

(iii)

The whole of the preceding argument is predicated on acceptance of what has been referred to as the principle of sufficient reason. Is such acceptance justified?

It has been argued by some that the principle is not only false but demonstrably false. It is logically impossible to explain *everything*, it is said – and this is most certainly true. Flew's exposition of the point has indeed been quoted at some length. And if this entails the falsity of the principle of sufficient reason, then that principle is most certainly false.

Yet none of this affects the argument developed above. For it is not predicated on acceptance of the principle in that sense. It is predicated on acceptance of what might be dubbed more generally the Explanatory Principle. According to this principle, one should press and go on pressing the question 'why' until it becomes clear that to press it any further is plain silly. Now what appears silly to one person may seem perfectly legitimate to another; but in all cases of dispute the proper procedure would appear to be to place upon opponents of these particular uses of 'why' the onus of giving reasons for its impropriety. For the best way of finding the limit of the application of 'why' is to question everything until either this is a self-evidently misguided procedure (in which case there will be no dispute), or good reason can be given for not doing so.

This interpretation of 'Explanatory Principle' is rather different from that given by N. Smart in *Philosophers and Religious Truth*, from which the term is borrowed. He argues that all contingent statements represent states of affairs which can be explained.[28] But this is going too far. It would mean for example that 'Why is it that a CEB exists?' (tenseless 'exists') would be a sensible question, and that 'that the CEB exists' (tenseless 'exists') could be explained. Or consider the statement 'Grass is green'. Is the greenness of grass explicable? Not really. It may be said that light waves of a certain length affect us in a certain way – but why in *that* way? It may be said that we are such that these particular waves affect us thus, and then a biological account may be given of why we are such. Yet this does not explain why we, who admittedly are such, experience these particular waves *thus*, as the colour *green*. The fact that we do experience them thus is surely, ultimately, inexplicable – something to be accepted with 'natural piety'. One of the difficulties with Whitehead's account is that by trying to explain *everything* in the world he ends up with the implausible doctrine of a bevy of transcendents, including for example the 'eternal object' green (rather like a Platonic form) which (crudely) is said to ingress into grass. Now if such a scheme could be made to work with regard to the nature of ingression, the ontological status of the eternal objects and the problem of whether they themselves call for further explanation, it would lay a strong claim on our credence (the principle of sufficient reason taking natural precedence over the law of parsimony). But since (it is here assumed) it cannot, and since no better alternative seems conceivable, questions about the greenness of grass tend to fizzle out, and rightly so. (Though this is not intended to imply that no one has any business to try and work out an explanation. Should an entirely novel theory be conceived, fair enough. The point is that it does not seem likely.) The situation thus parallels the one that would obtain if the postulation of a CEB led to an infinite regress or were otherwise hopelessly unacceptable.

Now in the case of tenseless world-contingency questions taken on their own, or the corresponding questions about why anything exists at all, good reasons can be given for supposing them to incorporate an illegitimate extension of the proper use of 'why'. In the case of the tensed world-contingency questions, on the other hand, no such reasons have been found. The questions appear to be perfectly in order (not, in Flew's acid phrase, a 'grammatically misleading expression of the will to profundity') and capable of being sensibly answered.[29] Therefore, other things being equal, the answer should, by the explanatory principle, be accepted.

Yet, it may be asked, why set so much store by squeezing as much use as possible out of 'why'? Granted it pays handsome dividends in the field of science and thereby justifies acceptance of the explanatory principle as a methodological tool of scientific inquiry; but what justification is there for elevating it into a metaphysical principle leading to the unverifiable and unfalsifiable postulation of a transcendent being?

Munitz indeed takes the objection still further. 'To appeal to the metaphysical Principle of Sufficient Reason . . . is already to commit oneself to the belief that the world's existence *can be explained*. The appeal to the metaphysical Principle of Sufficient

Reason, as a backing for the belief in a Necessary Being, is thus only a disguised way of affirming the belief itself.'[30] Such an extreme position is, however, untenable. It presupposes not only that there is a legitimate puzzle about the world's existence (and from Munitz's own analysis such legitimacy is not altogether clear, for he frequently gives the impression of unconsciously working on the basis of a silly interpretation of world-contingency questions) and that the notion of a Necessary Being is coherent, but that both are deducible from a metaphysical interpretation of the principle of sufficient reason. No such deduction can be made.

The less extreme objection merits considerable respect. The answer to the problem of the status of the explanatory principle depends in part on one's estimate of the character of the principle as adopted in scientific inquiry. Does it seem to spring from a drive for a certain kind of intelligibility only, or from a drive for intelligibility *tout court*? The answer surely is that it springs from the latter. We have noted that there are different kinds of explanation – but are we to suppose that they arise out of different drives for different kinds of intelligibility? It seems more plausible to suppose that they spring from one basic drive, and that the inquiry becomes diversified as the differing characters of the *explicanda* begin to stand out. On this view the principle of causality (as which the explanatory principle very often appears in a scientific context) is a comparatively narrow and specialised version of the explanatory principle, a particular channelling of the basic drive for intelligibility. The question then is whether the basic drive is to be trusted or whether it is only to be trusted in so far as it can be shown to be trustworthy; that is to say – as far as most opponents of its place in an argument from contingency are concerned, or in the most effective form of the objection – in so far as any explanatory hypothesis which it produces can or could in principle be verified or falsified empirically. And the answer to this is that the basic drive should be trusted – a contention which may be supported in two ways (and which thus goes beyond Martin's view, noted earlier, that satisfaction or dissatisfaction with contingency is 'a matter of temperament').

Firstly, we do in fact sometimes trust the drive even when verification or falsification is in principle impossible. Thus J. J.

C. Smart, who confesses to having been weaned from a too veri-
ficationist way of thinking, discusses the hypothesis (first introduced by Russell) that the universe began ten minutes before
the sentence now being read began to be written but with everything just as it was ten minutes ago. Here we have a hypothesis
which is incapable of empirical verification or falsification.
Now if the question is asked 'Why is the world as it is now?', the
hypothesis provides a logically immaculate reply. In that sense
it is intelligible. But does it satisfy the quest for intelligibility
from which the question arises? Not in the least. It presents us
with a complex and arbitrary primary collocation of world
items which cries out for further explanation. We are justified
therefore in rejecting it on the grounds of intelligibility alone –
that is to say, the basic drive for intelligibility is in this case
trusted even though it cannot finally be shown to be
trustworthy.[31]

This is not to deny of course that rejection of the hypothesis
may be reasoned. Indeed, it is to urge that such reasoning may
legitimately amount to a kind of falsification – even in a sense to
decisive falsification. But such falsification consists 'only' of
considerations of gains in intelligibility – it is 'soft' falsification
rather than the 'hard' kind advocated by proponents of the restricted scientific interpretation of the explanatory principle;
the point being that absence of the possibility of the 'hard' kind
of falsification or verification in connection with a particular
issue does not necessarily constitute a good reason for discon-
tinuing the quest for intelligibility with regard to that issue. A
different form of assessment may be appropriate.

The second point may be interpreted as a development of the
first. Even in science, if the adoption of a hypothesis resulted in
greater explanatory power, then in some cases at least it would
be worth adopting and should be adopted even if no series of ex-
periments could be devised which enabled the hypothesis to be
tested empirically, particularly if the impossibility were one in
principle. To some extent this view could be presented as a
straightforward appeal to individual opponents of the broader
interpretation of the explanatory principle to consider whether
they would in fact want to go as far as to maintain that a hypothesis should at no time be adopted in such circumstances; and
it may well be that they would not, in which case what they

would be doing would be trusting the basic drive for intelligibility. On the other hand, if they would go as far as this then it may be argued that such a stand is inconsistent with the view adopted in connection with the 'ten minutes ago hypothesis'. It would seem reasonable to extend the form of assessment adopted there to other issues and to accept or reject a hypothesis, particularly when empirical verification or falsification are in principle impossible, according as the reasoning in support of or in opposition to its explanatory claims appears sound.

What this implies is a broader acceptance of the propriety of subordinating the law of parsimony to the principle of sufficient reason. Where empirical verifcation or falsification is possible this is of course accepted practice – compare the micro-entities postulated in physics; but the suggestion here is that the practice may sometimes legitimately be maintained even when no such verification or falsification is possible.

Naturally, the alleged puzzle to be explained must be a genuine one. And one of the ways of showing that a given puzzle is genuine is to show that the questions expressing it are not silly and are capable of receiving a sensible answer. The attempt has been made here to do this with the tensed world-contingency questions.

If this broader and more flexible interpretation of the explanatory principle be accepted, no objection can be raised to its role in the argument from contingency which may then be accepted as a rightful part of a whole person's constant endeavour to make sense of the whole of his experience. As Owen remarks, 'the cosmological argument completes in its own mode the quest for intelligibility that prompts man throughout his intellectual activity (including his scientific investigations)'. The postulation of a CEB (Owen says 'God') is the 'fulfilment of human rationality'.[32] It would seem that if the argument be after all acceptable, rational theism is the ultimate rationalism. For as Whitehead observes: 'Rationalism is the belief that clarity can only be reached by pushing explanation to its utmost limits.' Yet the argument is not of course a strict or 'hard' proof in the old-time rationalist metaphysician's sense, and neither is there any question of its eliminating mystery. Rather does it respect a further dictum of Whitehead's, that 'the purpose of philosophy is not to . . . dissipate all mystery but to corner it'.[33]

It may be felt that in presenting this argument from contingency the lessons learned in Chapter 1 have been forgotten; that metaphysics has been divorced from religion and the experience of contingency from religious experience. After all, the *explicans* has hitherto consistently been referred to as a CEB rather than God, despite the obvious similarities.

The objection is sound but premature. In the next chapter the argument is rounded off by transforming what has hitherto been a metaphysical inquiry into an overtly religious one, the suggestion being that it is justifiable to identify the putative CEB with 'the God of religion'.

The concluding chapter, in the light of the argument of intervening chapters, will consider briefly whether belief in God is finally justified – for it should not be thought that the argument from contingency is the last word.

5 The Metaphysical Argument and Religion

(i) *Gods, God, and the CEB*

The term 'God of religion' is chosen for its imprecision and is intended to cover, let us say, the God of the Jews, that of Christians, that of Moslems, and perhaps that of Ramanuja's Hindu theism. For my first concern is to explore the possible connection between a metaphysical CEB and the theistic religions rather than a particular theistic religion. In the light of the discussion of Chapter 1 the possibility needs to be considered of connecting a metaphysical CEB with religious experience as found in a theistic context.

The obvious place to seek a link is in the experience of contingency which is a root of the movement of thought leading to a CEB. Let us suppose for a moment that the CEB does exist. In that case it is natural to reinterpret the experience of contingency as an experience of dependence – and the experience of dependence is of course a notable form of religious experience.

Now clearly we should not regard this new-found experience of dependence as a mere subjective experiencing-as. We should consider rather that we were now conscious of something that had been there all along without our noticing or acknowledging it; that, as it might be put, through the medium of a right interpretation of the world we were enabled to apprehend our direct relation to its (and our) sustainer, and react accordingly. Thus we should have a direct but mediate apprehension of the personal transcendent (as Trethowan, Mascall, Owen and others have put it).

Having proceeded thus far, however, it is virtually impossible to maintain an attitude of hard-boiled scepticism to other purported apprehensions of dependence on the personal transcendent. For if, as on the present hypothesis is believed, the personal transcendent is so to speak there to be apprehended, then just as we, prior to acceptance of our metaphysical argument were in direct relation to him, so too is everyone else. Why then should we deny other claims to have apprehended him? Because those who make them are not metaphysicians? Yet they may be, and in any case apprehension is not philosophy. Metaphysics may be needed to justify claims to apprehension, but there is no reason to suppose it necessary for apprehension itself. Because the interpretations mediating the putative apprehensions differ in certain respects from ours? Yet that need not invalidate the whole experience. If then we believe that the CEB exists, we should be inclined to regard favourably all (or most) claims to experience of dependence on a personal transcendent; and these of course tend to occur in the context of a religion.

Yet it is possible to go further than this. The experience of dependence relates to the CEB (or to God) as Creator; but the God of religion is more than Creator – he is the Supreme Being in the sense of being estimated worthy of worship. There are thus two basic and to some extent separable elements in the concept of God, and the former only has up to now featured conspicuously in the discussion of the CEB. If the notion of a CEB is to be closely assimilated to that of the God of religion, it needs further development so that the experience of dependence may be accompanied by an attitude of worship.

The seed of such development lies in the earlier argument to the effect that the CEB is good. The thesis that he is good may be developed in two ways, and when this is done the relation between the CEB and the God of religion is close indeed.

In the first place it was argued earlier that the CEB has existed (if at all) for an infinite duration. It would now seem plausible to suggest that he *will* exist for an infinite duration also. For a self-creating being who is good may be expected to continue to create himself a good being – that is the kind of attraction which goodness exercises over a good being – and as good he will have no motive to cease to be; moreover he will not just happen to cease to be for he has power over his existence.

Yet what if he is not very good? This leads to the second development. He must be more good than not to create us, and sufficiently stably good to sustain us. But more; again, goodness exercising the attraction it does, a being with such a degree of goodness and with the power to create himself would presumably create himself to be as good as possible – and what are the limits of such possibility to a being with such power? It is arguable therefore that the CEB is not only eternal (in the sense of temporally infinite) but also perfect and incorruptible.

The notion of perfection is itself no doubt vague, prompting the question 'Perfect in which way or ways?' Yet the basis of the ascription of goodness to a putative CEB is our estimation of the goodness of the cosmos as an environment in which life may be enjoyed and valued. And since the corner-stone of a satisfactory life at the human level may in general be said to be love, it appears sensible to suppose that the creation of the cosmos is an act of love, and the Supreme Being perfect in love. (Though doubtless other elements might be added.)

Now if this further development of the notion of a CEB be seriously entertained, what reaction does it evoke? What if not gratitude, humility, praise, reverence? An attitude which at the very least must tremble on the brink of worship and which in the context of, let us say, the ritual and developed doctrinal elements in a given theistic religion would most surely become worship.

Again, as in the case of the experience of dependence, once we proceed as far as this it is impossible not to concede a certain validity to worship-experiences as these are found in the religions of the world. Clearly, therefore, impressive links may be forged between the metaphysical argument from contingency and religious theism in a way which appears to favour the modulation of the metaphysical conclusion into an overtly religious one.

Yet religious experience is not just a question of claims to apprehend God. It is a question too of claims that God has positively revealed himself. Now it is not inconceivable that the CEB should exist, that he should have been apprehended as in theistic religion he is claimed to have been apprehended, but that he should never have revealed himself positively. Yet if he is at all as conceived above, that is to say, motivated by love, the notion of his positively revealing himself is not in the least implausible. On the contrary it fits into the picture nicely. And when this is considered, and in addition that although our notion of a CEB has been developed in a metaphysical context, it is clearly overwhelmingly influenced by a concept of God developed in a religious context so that the metaphysician is indebted to religion, then it seems exaggeratedly negative resolutely to reject the notion of revelation altogether. For again, in the outstanding cases claims to apprehension of a personal transcendent and revelation-claims are inseparable. Moreover the sheer existence of the world, bearing witness as it does (on the hypothesis being considered) to a personal creator, is a form of self-disclosure of that being so that there is no real gap or strict boundary between claims to apprehension and revelation-claims; for revelation is special self-disclosure.

If then we believed in the CEB described above, we should find ourselves interpreting life religiously, not just metaphysically. Belief in such a personal transcendent would arouse feelings and emotions akin to if not identical with those found in living religions, though the doctrinal aspect of this 'individual religion' would have a low degree of ramification. It would appear plausible therefore to suppose that the CEB to which metaphysical analysis points is the God of religion approached from a particular angle. And although the 'God of religion' is several Gods of several religions, it would appear plausible to suppose that the different theistic religions are in fact all centred on experience of one personal transcendent being.

But where then does the truth lie? Which notion of God is to be taken to approximate most closely to his nature? Or where should one suppose that God has most fully revealed himself? And what is to be made of the non-theistic or non-monotheistic religions?

Taking the last question first, it is feasible to suggest a theistic interpretation of all religious experience. This line is taken for example by H. H. Farmer and by H. D. Lewis, and the thesis is argued in a rather different way by N. Smart. He distinguishes two main strands of religious experience, the numinous and the mystical. With regard to the latter there is on his view no problem here, for he argues persuasively that mystical experience is susceptible of either a non-theistic or a theistic interpretation. As for the sense of the numinous it finds its most intense expression in a fully-fledged theism (though it may occur in a polytheistic context) and hence there is no problem there either. Thus theism is able to do full justice to both main strands in the sense of allowing a certain harmonic validity to both. Indeed, it alone is able to do full justice to both, for, he argues, of the other two main types of doctrinal system other than theism, represented for example by the agnosticism of the Theravada on the one hand and the Advaita Vedanta of Shan-kara on the other, the former has no proper place for the numin-ous strand, and the latter relegates it to an inferior position, the idea of a personal God being thought to be ultimately illusory.[1] Thus the considerations involved in Smart's 'natural theology of religious experience' fit in well with the notion of an omnipre-sent God, with a God of love moreover who might be expected to reveal himself to some extent everywhere.

What then of the previous question as to where one should suppose that God has most fully revealed himself? Clearly in the first instance at least it is necessary to refer here to the im-portant figures of religious history, for he is unlikely to have re-vealed himself most fully to someone whom the revelation affected in such a way as not to affect others and thereby make a mark. Such a revelation would be self-defeating, and the notion of a content of revelation which is not widely proclaimed is inherently implausible. As Smart has urged, it is wise to base important truths of religion not on 'my feeble intuitions or my neighbour's faltering visions' but on, for example, such 'ex-plosively numinous' experiences as those of Jeremiah.[2]

If we do turn to the important figures, what is to be said? In the first place there is a general argument in favour of Jesus to the effect that since the idea of God which has most influenced the course of the argument from contingency is one developed mainly in a Christian setting, it is both natural and prima facie plausible to suppose that if God there be, it is in such a setting that he has most fully revealed himself. The alternative is to suppose that although God is (broadly speaking) as Christians claim him to be, he has revealed himself more fully in an other than Christian way, that is to say, that Christians have acciden-tally stumbled closer to the truth than those to whom he has indeed revealed himself. One is reminded of Farrer's remark about Copernicus and the sun-worshippers. It seems more sen-sible to take the fruitful interplay between metaphysics and

Christian theology as being of some significance with regard to the validity of specifically *Christian* theism.

Yet this general consideration needs to be supplemented with rather more specific reference to Jesus if there is to be any hope of showing positively that the relation between Christianity and the truth about God is not in fact merely accidental. For the argument from contingency is in the main dependent on aspects of the Christian understanding of God which developed in the general setting of Christian thought and experience, rather than being due directly to Jesus himself and his proclamation; indeed, it is fundamentally dependent on a specifically Christian setting only in so far as one's understanding of perfection relies on Jesus. Moreover, as will be seen, more specific reference to an individual religious leader is vital if there is to be any hope of showing positively that special revelation has in fact occurred, rather than assuming that because it fits.in with the notion of a loving God it must have occurred.

Now there is clearly very great room for discussion here. Smart, for example, argues that a reason for choosing specifically Christian theism among the theistic alternatives is that Christ is both man and God and hence is able to effect that salvation, need for which arises from man's sense of sin and inadequacy engendered by his confrontation with the majesty and holiness of God.[3] Yet this argument is valid only (a) if it makes sense to say that Jesus is (was) both God and man; (b) if there is good reason to suppose that he is both God and man; (c) if it makes sense to say that incarnation solves the problem occasioned by man's sin; and (d) if the problem is of a kind needing to be solved by an incarnation alone rather than some other alternative. The first two of these are highly questionable; the latter two lead to a discussion of the nature of atonement.

While it is impossible to delve deeply into these issues here, it may be urged in connection with the latter that the essence of the Gospel is not that God looks to man to make himself acceptable and, since he is unable to do this, does it for him vicariously and lovingly in Christ. Rather is it that God accepts the unacceptable on the sole condition of their being willing to be accepted. That is to say, we have to learn to accept being accepted despite being unacceptable as part of the love of God. His acceptance of us is not conditional upon a unique act of atonement in the sense that, had that act not occurred, he would have been unable to accept us.

Yet if this view be adopted, the repercussions on the notion of incarnation are considerable; for it means in effect that his acceptance of us is not conditional upon an incarnation. Even if it could make sense to say that Jesus was both man and God, there is no religious need to suppose him to have been both, for there was (is) nothing needing to be done, in respect either of his acceptance of us or of our acceptance of his acceptance of us, that only Jesus the God-man could have done and not Jesus the extraordinary man or (human) medium of revelation. It follows, since there is no real historical evidence which needs to be accounted for in terms of the divinity of Jesus, that attempts to make sense of the Chalcedonian formula that he is 'at once complete in Godhead and complete in manhood' are superfluous – except as exercises in doctrinal history or in tracing the significance of outdated and misleading credal statements.

This approach to the significance of Jesus will therefore not do. What of the approach which fastens on him as the supreme human witness to God? Here historical and moral factors feature largely.

With regard to the historical factors it is argued by some that the historical Jesus is of little significance in comparison with the Christ of the Kerygma. Yet questions as to the nature of Jesus's person and teaching are not lightly to be brushed aside, as the post-Bultmannian concern for the historical Jesus shows. Do any results of this quest support the view of Jesus as the supreme witness and most significant locus of special revelation?

Ones which may be seen as of particular interest are J. Jeremias's findings concerning Jesus's use of 'Abba'. According to Jeremias, although in Palestinian Judaism God is addressed as father in liturgical prayers, (a) Hebrew is used, the sacred language; (b) the address 'Our Father' is part of a twin address, 'Our Father, Our King', where God's majesty as a king is underscored as much as or even more than his fatherhood; (c) it is the community as a whole which so addresses him. 'To date nobody has produced one single instance in Palestinian Judaism where God is addressed as 'my Father' by an individual person. . . . But Jesus did just this. To his disciples it must have been something quite extraordinary.' Yet it is attested by all four gospels, particularly in connection with his prayers (the one exception being Mark 15:34, par. Matthew 27:46).[4]

The word for 'father' used by Jesus was the Aramaic word 'Abba' and this too is of tremendous significance, being 'without analogy in Jewish prayers of the first millennium A.D.'. Thus 'Jewish prayers on the one hand do not contain a single example of "abba" as an address for God; Jesus on the other hand always used it when he prayed (with the exception of the cry from the cross, Mark 15:34). This means that we here have an unequivocal characteristic of the unique way in which Jesus expressed himself, of his *ipsissima vox*.'[5]

Now 'abba' was originally the word used by babies, and although by the time of Jesus it would be used by grown-up sons and daughters, to a Jewish mind it would have been irreverent and therefore unthinkable to call God by such a familiar word. 'It was something new, something unique and unheard of, that Jesus dared to take this step and to speak with God as a child speaks with his father, simply, intimately, securely. There is no doubt then that the "Abba" which Jesus uses to address God reveals the very basis of his communion with God.'[6]

Apart from the context of prayers Jesus uses 'Abba' for God one hundred and forty-two times in the Gospels, and at first sight it seems to be *the* designation for God on his lips. Yet this is misleading, for one hundred of the uses occur in John's Gospel and thirty-one in the special Matthean source. Thus in the earliest traditions, Mark, Q and L, Jesus uses it only rarely, apparently on special occasions. But why?

Here 'one has to know that the father–son comparison is familiar to Palestinian apocalyptic as an illustration of how revelation is transmitted'. Its use by Jesus is foreshadowed only within the context of messianic expectation:

Thus, when Jesus spoke of God as 'my Father' he was referring not to a familiarity and intimacy with God available to anyone, but to a unique revelation which was bestowed upon him. He bases his authority on the fact that God has graciously endowed him with the full revelation, revealing himself to him as only a father can reveal himself to his son.

'Abba', then, is a word which conveys revelation. It represents the centre of Jesus's awareness of his mission (*Sendungsbewusstsein*).[7]

In the light of this the Lord's Prayer would appear to be an authorising of the disciples by Jesus to use 'Abba' too; the shorter and therefore older version of the prayer (Luke 11:2–4, cf. Matthew 6:9–13) beginning, not 'Our Father', but 'Father', that is, 'Pater' or 'Abba'. ('Shorter and therefore older' because no one would have dared to shorten such a central text.)

Jeremias's conclusion is that 'Abba' as an address to God is an authentic utterance of Jesus, implying the claim of a unique revelation and a unique authority. 'With "Abba" we are behind the Kerygma. We are confronted with something new and unheard of which breaks through the limits of Judaism. Here we see who the historical Jesus was: the man who had the power to address God as "Abba" and who included the sinners and the publicans in the kingdom by authorising them to repeat this one word, "Abba, dear Father".'[8]

The relevance of these researches to the problem in hand lies first of all, fairly obviously, in the fact that we seem to be in touch with the historical Jesus. But secondly it lies in the fact that the message of this Jesus is morally inspiring and spiritually significant. And thirdly it lies in the fact that the historical Jesus is revealed as one whose authority (attested throughout the Gospels) is rooted in an intense experience of special intimacy with God. Now claims to such intimacy seem in themselves arrogant indeed, yet in this case seem to have blended harmoniously with a didactic insistence on humility which in turn seems to have been exemplified in the character of the teacher. The total impact of this man appears in consequence very striking indeed. If God there be, a God to be worshipped, who has somewhere revealed himself, Jesus's claims to be the focal point of that revelation are most impressive.

Along such lines as these it may be urged that the antecedent plausibility of the fullest revelation lying in *Christian* theism is supported with specific reference to Jesus. Yet the outline only of the justification is sketched here. It is impossible to deal adequately in the present context with the objections of a Moslem, for example, who would presumably argue that while God is perfect the notion of perfection entertained by Christians is inferior to that entertained in Islam, and that the view of Jesus as more morally admirable or spiritually significant than Muhammad must be rejected utterly. The criteria of judgement in this field are complex and debatable. Yet judgement is and must be exercised; and the present judgement, all too briefly and dogmatically asserted here, is that among the theistic alternatives Christian theism has most to be said in its favour.

Before leaving the topic, however, it is necessary to develop one of the points made above as it is open to misunderstanding. It may be thought that part of the argument is that since Jesus made such arrogant claims about enjoying an intimate relationship with God, and yet preached and, as far as we are able to judge, practised humility, the only plausible explanation of this psychological anomaly is that he was in fact in communion with God. Yet this is not the argument; and if it were it would be entirely unacceptable because it goes against the methodological postulate that a natural explanation of events in the world is always in principle possible.

On the other hand, while this postulate proscribes certain ways of justifying belief in God, if this belief can be justified in other ways without running counter to the postulate, it is necessary to add a rider to the postulate which would permit an argument similar to the unacceptable one, yet one which is methodologically sound. The rider is that the principle of natural explanation must not be held to rule out completely the very possibility of God's acting *in* the world (as opposed to acting *on* it by sustaining it). Such a prohibition is religiously quite unacceptable, for it is of the essence of religious theism that God has acted and does act, that there is divine initiative in history – for example in special revelation. If he be not part-cause of revelation, then revelation-claims are exposed to the debunking charge of mere subjectivity.

Now it may be felt that this notion contradicts the principle of natural explanation, but in fact the two may be harmonised. For the principle may be modified to allow the possibility of direct divine 'causal' action on individuals in the world, provided that this action is such that it may be ignored by the scientist (whether physicist, biologist, psychologist or whatever).

That is to say, for all practical, naturalistic scientific purposes there is no direct divine action; but in fact (on this view) there is such action (though perhaps more in the psychological realm than in the physical – in events like Jesus's sense of vocation rather than an alleged walking on water), and from the religious point of view it is crucial. But, it must be again insisted, the religious point of view cannot be justified by appeal to such action. For even if by adopting the principle of natural explanation (and Occam's razor) one runs the risk of misinterpreting genuine divine action in the world, the grounds on which the principles are adopted seem virtually unassailable and no satisfactory alternatives have been suggested. It is necessary to risk excluding too much in order to avoid being overwhelmed by the inclusion of a multitude of incompatibles.[9]

Bergson wrote: 'The forceps of the mind are crude with which to grasp reality.' According to the modified view the naturalistic forceps are sufficiently delicate to manage reality sensibly and intelligibly, but insufficiently delicate to manage it *comme il faut*. For that supernaturalistic forceps are required; though the need may be far from obvious, and within the limits of a purely scientific naturalism is indeed strictly superfluous.

The argument concerning the significance of Jesus may now be expressed more lucidly. *Given* belief in the existence of God, and *given* the possibility of a limited direct action by him on individuals, *then* it is legitimate to cast around among candidates for revelationary ultimacy to see whether there is any feature of a given individual's spiritual life (in a broader sense, including for example teaching) which might be more illumined than any features in other individuals' spiritual lives by supposing that it is in part due to divine initiative. Indeed, if no such features were to be found anywhere, the presumption would be that God had not after all revealed himself. Yet in the case of Jesus such a feature is to be found. Thus acceptance of the rider permits direct justification of belief in special revelation, and identification of the relevant feature(s) permits identification of its locus.

The preceding account of divine action in the world follows of course from the view that appeals to miracles as a justification of belief are completely unfounded – a view enshrined in the naturalistic methodological postulate. Yet the essential tenet is safeguarded that God acts in history in a way that may become apparent to the discerning believer. It does not then matter if an event or pattern of events has in a sense to be seen-as revelation, for that particular seeing-as may well be, within its theistic frame of reference, as justified as its naturalistic counterpart within the non-theistic and non-religious frame of reference of, for example, science. That is to say, it may be a way of becoming aware of a dimension of activity to which the non-theistic seer-as is blind.

Yet 'seeing-as' (or 'experiencing-as') is misleading in this respect. For in a classic case of seeing-as, such as the faces –goblet puzzle picture, there is no 'extra' line in one of the interpretations corresponding to the extra dimension of activity apprehended in the theistic interpretation. It is impossible therefore to say that either the goblet or the faces interpretation is the *correct* one. In the theistic–atheistic case, however (the atheistic case being here intended to be distinguished sharply from the non-theistic case of, for example, the scientist, who as a scientist is a non-theist only in the sense that his field of study is restricted to the cosmos *qua* natural), the whole point is that both sides do claim to be correct. And what makes one of them correct is precisely the presence or absence in reality of the 'extra' dimension of activity. It is lack of reference to this extra dimension and to the ultimate non-parallelism between seeing-as in the puzzle picture case and seeing-as in the revelation case that constitutes one of the principal weaknesses of Hick's and other similar accounts of the interpretative activity of theists.

The view taken here then is that the CEB of the argument from contingency may legitimately be identified with the God of religion and with the God of the Christian religion in particular. Should the conclusion be drawn on the basis of the arguments up to this point that a rational justification of Christian theism is after all possible? Tentatively it may be affirmed that it may. Yet as mentioned earlier, it should not be thought that the argument from contingency is the last word. Before a judgement as to whether belief in God is finally justified may be attempted, it will be necessary to throw more light on the character of the putative justification as well as indicating briefly further aspects of its total structure.

(ii) *The Argument from Contingency as an Argument from Religious Experience*

The argument of the preceding chapters followed naturally from the discussion of religious experience in Chapter 1, at the end of which hopes were expressed for a possible threefold advantage attending a successful argument for the existence of God rooted in religious experience of some kind. It is necessary to ask whether these hopes have been fulfilled, and if not, whether the failure is serious.

Firstly, the hope that the gap between the entity reached by argument and the God of religion would be narrowed by basing the argument in religious experience of some kind has not been fulfilled to the extent that it might have been had it been possible to base the argument on a form of religious experience$_1$ rather than on an experience which is not initially religious in character at all. On the other hand, the course taken by the argument has justified not only reinterpreting the experience of contingency as a religious experience of dependence, but also relating it intimately to the religious experiences of worship, praise, reverence – indeed to the whole spectrum of religious experience$_1$ and revelation. In addition we have seen that there are no real difficulties in marrying the CEB with different doctrinal schemes so that the gap between the CEB and the God of religion is not a real problem. Moreover there are methodological considerations militating against expectation of a complete harmony between the entity reached by a comparatively limited argument such as the argument from contingency and the God of a given religion, for the concept of the latter is in every case a highly ramified concept embedded in a complex doctrinal scheme which no argument from contingency should be expected to validate *in toto*.

Secondly, assuming the argument to be sound, are the valid grounds for belief in God's existence different from the grounds on which the world has come to believe? In a sense yes, for the kind of analysis of contingency presented here, along with the argument based upon it, have hardly been principal moving forces in the lives of the majority of believers. Yet in a sense no, for the analysis given is but a refinement of an original experience or family of experiences which surely have featured significantly in inducing or buttressing belief in God, and it is plausible to consider the argument as a refinement of a kind of thinking not infrequently exercised at a more primitive level in connection with such experiences. Thus it is not the case that what is accepted here as a philosophically valid ground of belief is a movement of thought radically different from the movement of thought of countless unsophisticated believers in the way that, to take Farrer's example, Copernicus's train of thought was radically different from those of sun-worshippers, or, we might add, Kepler's mathematical reasoning was from his sun-worship.[10] Nor is it the case that, in Baillie's words, it is 'an accident of coincidence that there is anything in the world's faith at all', belief in God having had 'no solid basis in the soul's experience'. That would be so only if (a) God existed; (b) people believed in him on the basis of supposed experiences of him; and (c) the proper grounds of belief in him excluded experiences of him. The view defended here does not deny that individuals experience God, does not deny that such experiences are relevant factors in belief, and does not affirm that ultimately the valid ground of belief is something wholly unrelated.

Moreover the notion of a 'valid ground' of belief must be contextualised. A putative apprehension of dependence on a personal transcendent is not a valid ground of belief for the contemporary philosopher of religion, knowing what he does about rival experiences and so on; yet for someone like an unsophisticated nomad it may be perfectly valid, for he may well have no valid grounds for scepticism regarding such experiences, in which case he has every right to trust them as epistemologically comparable with experiences of the external world. Thus the position may be that (a) God exists; (b) he is apprehended by a number of individuals; (c) for many of these individuals their own putative apprehensions of him (or, for many others, their reports of them) are valid grounds of belief in him; (d) for others, and for progressively more due to increases in both education and knowledge, their own putative apprehensions (or reports of other people's apprehensions) need to be supplemented by arguments to show that they are genuine apprehensions. It follows that the necessity of an argument from contingency or something like it today does not render either previous belief superstitious or present experience redundant.

The second hoped-for advantage of an argument rooted in religious experience of some kind may be said to have materialised to a satisfactory extent.

Thirdly, does the argument after all 'touch our feelings' or does it remain a 'mere speculative argument', 'external' in the sense of being a piece of cold metaphysics incapable of or ineffectual in rousing a warm religious glow? Inevitably the answer must vary from one individual to the next. Yet it is arguable that with its constant implied appeal to the reader to scrutinise the character of all his continuing experience of the world, and with its insistence on the links between the reinterpreted experience of contingency and the whole spectrum of religious experiences, there is perhaps rather more emphasis on full-blooded personal involvement in the argument than is customarily the case with cosmological-type arguments, thereby significantly weakening the 'ballet of bloodless categories' objection. Moreover this feature of the argument will be reinforced in practice when it is taken to its full conclusion in the final chapter.

It may be concluded that the soft argument from contingency goes a long way towards living up to the hopes entertained for a successful argument rooted in some form of religious experience, and that in so far as it fails to do so the failure is not serious. For perhaps only an argument rooted in religious experience$_1$ could completely live up to these hopes. Yet such an argument is not available. The argument from contingency is the only sound argument from religious experience.

Yet it would be premature to claim that the argument presented is as 'full-blooded' as any successful argument for the existence of God is likely to be. This may be true of the argument or body of arguments as finally adumbrated; but its total structure has yet to be indicated.

6 Contingency and Cosmic Teleology

It is customary to contrast cosmological-type arguments with teleological-type arguments. The most useful distinction to be made here is perhaps indicated by speaking with T. Penelhum of Existential and Qualitative arguments.[1] The former are concerned with the problem that there is a world at all; the latter with problems regarding the kind of world that is, problems not only of order but of value, meaning and so on. The soft argument from contingency is an Existential argument even though contingency may in a sense be said to be a kind of quality, for it deals with the 'quality' of *existence* rather than with the *qualities* of existence.

Now it is a feature of the soft argument that, unlike traditional Existential arguments, it does appeal at crucial points to qualities of the world and human existence. This happens especially when grounds are adduced for supposing the CEB to be good. Yet this does not mean that the argument becomes either illicitly or covertly a Qualitative one, thereby perhaps compromising itself. In a manner shortly to be elucidated, qualitative considerations may be deployed in a subsidiary or dependent *quasi*-cosmic teleological argument designed to show that a comparatively characterless CEB posited on other grounds, for example of explanatory ultimacy in connection with contingency, is qualitatively 'this' rather than 'that'. There is nothing of an illicit or compromising nature, however, in thus allowing qualitative features to function as evidence for rounding out the character of a CEB; for, as urged earlier, if there is reason to suppose him to exist it is justifiable to judge his character in the light of his creation.

Yet what of the possibility of an independent Qualitative argument for the existence of God? The question must be asked despite Hume and his successors, for the traditional influence of the Existential arguments has been found to be not entirely unwarranted, and the same might prove true of the influence of Qualitative arguments.

Brief reference was made at the beginning to the possibility of appealing to moral data, and there would appear to be no likelihood of any such argument succeeding. Similarly with various arguments from religious experience (that is, religious experience$_1$) and from questions about the meaning of life. Again, the once-popular arguments from striking and apparently inexplicable instances of adaptation in evolution have died under the influence of naturalistic evolutionary theories (though their ghosts survive), and it is urged here that whatever the merits or demerits of any particular evolutionary theory, such theistic arguments are methodologically corrupt by virtue of contravening the principle of natural explanation. This applies equally to any attempt to explain theologically the emergence of life from matter, or mind from its pre-mental matrix, or the kind of scientific data adduced by advocates of some kind of 'immanent teleology', for example by E. E. Harris in his impressive *The Foundations of Metaphysics in Science.*[2]

There remains the kind of broad teleological argument of which Whitehead's system is a rather special case. It may be admitted that, were there good reason for supposing the world to be as described by Whitehead, it would be necessary to introduce God in order to furnish complete intelligibility. The question arises whether a sound argument of the broad teleological type can be formulated in a non-Whiteheadian context – perhaps the outstanding attempt at such a formulation being Tennant's.

The initial move of any cosmic teleological argument will almost certainly be concerned with the problem of order, either with the fact that the world has any degree of order, or with its alleged high degree of order. In both cases the assumption tends to be made that there is a similarity of degree of order between all other parts of the cosmos and those hitherto accessible to human investigation – a not unreasonable supposition in view of the absence of any indication to the contrary in the expanding circle of knowledge of the cosmos, though it is not absolutely necessary for the argument, as in any case the undeniable and impressive order in the local part of the universe continues to call for consideration. In both cases the question is raised whether an orderer needs to be invoked in order to account for the order.

It would be tedious as well as unnecessary to rehearse in detail the several Humean replies to this. Yet they must not be omitted entirely, and some at least can still benefit from further elucidation in connection with comparatively recent arguments like Tennant's.

The objection that cosmic design might be the work of a group of beings rather than of one may be met by an appeal to Occam's razor. The objection that in virtue of the uniqueness of the cosmos there can be no probability of its being designed may be met, either by conceding the point but declaring it irrelevant, since the notion of probability can be replaced here perfectly satisfactorily by the notion of plausibility, or else by urging that the objection relies on an unacceptably narrow understanding of the concept of probability. Rather than get involved in an analysis of the concept of probability I am content to adopt the former alternative here. Two other objections also retain their force, namely (*a*) that if there is to be a cosmos at all (and if this is questioned, the move is made from Qualitative to Existential considerations) it must possess some degree of order and to that extent resemble a product of design; and (*b*) that the argument could only justify belief in a cosmic artisan and not a divine creator. The latter is impugned by Tennant who argues that the designer of the cosmos could not be its architect without also being its creator, on the ground that

> we cannot entertain the supposition that the linkages, interactions, and relations of pre-existent but 'chaotic' – i.e. relatively orderless – things could be stripped from them or from their determinate natures, leaving them unannihilated, and new linkages, such as should make a cosmos, could be superimposed on them, leaving those natures unaltered. [It is] the natures of the existents that prescribe or define their possible rapport; and neither the existent nor its rapport is separable from the other without the annihilation of both.[3]

Yet while this may be granted, it does not rule out the possibilities either of an architect's exercising an everlasting ordering influence on an everlastingly ordered cosmos, or of his *gradually* bringing order out of a relatively orderless state. According to Tennant, 'the universe has no environment to evoke from it the epigenetic, or what may be called the emergent'; yet a cosmic architect would constitute such an environment, and order could be an induced emergent consequent of chaos (or, in view of objection (*a*), of near-chaos).[4] Objection (*b*) therefore stands.

Two other objections are more important. The first concerns infinite explanatory escalation. According to Hume the postulation of divine mental order to account for cosmic order initiates a vicious infinite regress. This objection might be met in part by the defence of a concept of deity as an explanatory ultimate; but in order to be fully satisfactory the defence would have to involve reference to the argument from contingency and consequently the teleological argument would fail as an independent argument – though it might succeed in so far as it centred on the concept of purpose as an explanatory ultimate. Yet even so, if, instructively, the main thrust of the objection is taken to concern the initiation of a vicious infinite qualitative regress, then it retains considerable force. For it is as logically permissible to ask why a putative CEB – or, better, COEB, 'Cosmos-Order-Explaining-Being'– is such as to be capable of ordering the cosmos as it is to ask why the cosmos is ordered; and the former question, unlike the question as to why the CEB exists (tensed 'exists'), does not forestall a vicious infinite regress by fizzling out. In this respect the argument from contingency appears to hold a monopoly. Certainly any move towards a cosmic teleological argument is accordingly hampered, though not as it turns out completely blocked, by considerations of parsimony.

Such flickering hope as may remain for an independent argument of this kind is extinguished, however, by the further and principal objection that the cosmos may be compared as well with (on the macroscopic and microscopic scales respectively) a vegetable or an atom as with a product of design. This removes the ground from beneath any advocate of the need for a divine designer, even if with Plantinga and others we have to admit, as we surely do, that there is indeed *some* force in the teleological argument as an analogical inference, on the ground that while the universe is comparable with a vegetable it is also in certain important respects comparable with things we know to be designed. Despite this – which needs to be emphasised and which in due course will be assigned a place in the overall structure of a possible justification of theism – the objection is decisive; for its force is that the latter analogy, the comparison of the cosmos with things we know to be designed, is insufficiently impressive to prevent fidelity to Occam's razor from ensuring that it is subordinated to the comparison with a vegetable or an atom. (Plantinga unfortunately seems open to the charge of infidelity.[5]) Although, therefore, Hume may be said to have starved the argument into submission rather than delivered the *coup de grâce* as is frequently supposed, in submission it remains.

Thus when Tennant for example is bemused by the 'conspiration of innumerable causes to produce, by their united and reciprocal action, and to maintain, a general order of Nature', he makes too light of the explanatory possibility of the general order being due to some systematising influence of the cosmos in its function as a whole on its parts; and it is highly interesting in this respect that Whitehead should have recommended F. S. C. Northrop's doctrine of the cosmos as a 'macroscopic atom' exercising just such an influence as the only alternative to his own theory of 'microscopic atomic occasions.'[6] Tennant argues that 'no *explanation* is contained in the assertion that the world is an organic whole and consequently involves adaptiveness. That is only a restatement of the occult and wondrous fact that cries for explanation.' In other words it is necessary to press a question such as the following: Why is the cosmos this kind of macroscopic atom or organic whole, when it conceivably might have been a less determinate near-chaos 'in which similar events never occurred, none recurred, universals had no place, relations no fixity, things no nexus of determination, and "real" categories no foothold'?[7] Yet the matter is rather more complex than Tennant's account suggests, for this question, which may be dubbed a 'cosmic teleological question', is susceptible of two interpretations analogous to the dual interpretations of world-contingency questions. And, not unnaturally, the different interpretations are related to not one but two different 'occult and wondrous' facts allegedly crying for explanation; though once the distinctions are clarified the crying in any case has to stop.

If 'is' in 'Why is . . .?' is *tensed*, the question, unlike tensed world-contingency questions, may be answered by reference to prior states of the cosmos. Either it has always been in a similar degree of order or, better perhaps, operated according to similar natural laws; or it has evolved from other degrees of order in other 'cosmic epochs' (Whitehead), in which case there is no reason to suppose that the evolution was anything other than natural. One might perhaps ask why the present cosmic epoch has lasted as long as it has – why, that is, the present degree of order has the degree of temporal stability that it has – but since there is no way of assessing what counts as a reasonable duration for a cosmic epoch, this consideration is at best inconclusive (though, taken in conjunction with tensed world-contingency questions, it may have confirmatory value in the general way to be indicated shortly). On the whole it would appear that Flew's advocacy of Stratonician atheism is in this case, that is, with regard to an independent teleological argument, exemplary.

On the other hand, if 'is' in 'Why is . . .?' is *tenseless* – and this is the interpretation which gets to the heart of Tennant's contention – the question may be answered by pointing out that, other things being equal, in a single throw of dice (corresponding to the existence of the universe) the occurrence of a double five (corresponding to a high degree of order) should be no more perplexing than would have been the occurrence of any other combination (corresponding to lower or higher degrees of order). Therefore, *pace* Tennant (who himself, as will be seen shortly, draws the analogy between the existence of the cosmos and a single throw of dice but fails to follow through its implications), although the assertion that the world is an organic whole may be the expression of an occult and wondrous fact, this fact does not even mumble, let alone cry out for explanation. The point about the single throw of dice combines with the point about explanatory escalation to render this tenseless question silly in the way that the proper analysis of explanation renders tenseless world-contingency questions silly.

The importance of drawing this distinction between tensed and tenseless cosmic teleological questions may be further emphasised by considering N. Smart's discussion of cosmic teleology. Like Tennant he mistakenly regards the high degree of orderliness in the cosmos as a genuine rather than 'silly' problem. But, further, he urges that an explanation of the present order of the world in terms of preceding states of (possibly lesser degrees of) order of the world is not a finally satisfactory explanation. Consequently there is need for an explanation of the ordered cosmos as a whole.[8] Now the notion of the cosmos 'as a whole' here clearly covers the whole temporal span of the cosmos, its total 'tenseless' existence. Thus, as with Tennant, Smart's understanding of the basic teleological problem would be best expressed in terms of the tenseless cosmic teleological question. This being so, it is not surprising that the explanation in terms of preceding cosmic states is found unsatisfactory, for it is intended to cope with the quite different tensed cosmic teleological question. Failure to distinguish the two questions is in this case clearly misleading. Once the distinction is made, the explanation in terms of preceding cosmic states is seen to be perfectly satisfactory in its proper context. (Incidentally, Smart insists (4.48) that the request for an explanation of the ordered cosmos as a whole should be related to his earlier request for an explanation of the existence of the cosmos as a whole. In view of the meaning of 'cosmos as a whole' in this context it would appear that his earlier argument from contingency is after all based on a silly interpretation of world-contingency questions.)

It should be added that the preceding criticisms of cosmic teleology hold except in idiosyncratic cases like panpsychism, where the interpretation of the ordered constituents of the cosmos, combined with a refusal to treat the cosmos itself as a complex actual entity, necessitates the introduction of a cosmic co-ordinator. (Hence the insertion of the condition 'other things being equal' when replying to the tenseless cosmic teleology question.) Another example would be the combination of ontological pluralism with a strict doctrine of external relations – one thinks of Leibnitz. It follows that the postulate of cosmic teleology does not permit simple dismissal by appeal to a general principle as in Flew's appeal to the Stratonician principle. As observed in connection with the argument from contingency, that appeal is eminently sound provided only that no characteristic of the universe thought to be discerned refuses to be unproblematic. Most do not; but some do, for example contingency and panpsychism. It is necessary to treat awkward cases on their individual merits.

Two further points need to be made. The first is that in the panpsychism case the problem of order is so acute that the introduction of a cosmic co-ordinator seems justified despite the ensuing logical invitation to an explanatory spiral. Once again the Explanatory Principle is given precedence over Occam's razor. Once again the need appears for delicate balancing of principles and other considerations in making a rational judgement (in this case the 'other considerations' would include an assessment of the evidence supporting and opposing a panpsychist interpretation of the cosmos). There is no straightforward knockdown logical veto or proof.

The second point is that although it is dubious whether the existence of a deity could ever be said to be probable, circumstances are conceivable in which it could be said to be plausible. The fact that there is of necessity only one universe functions importantly in objections to cosmic teleology (as in the remark about a single throw of dice) but it does not proscribe it utterly. 'The mere fact that a thing is unique does not of course entail that it has no property in common with anything else. The fact that the universe is single or unique, therefore, does not invalidate the argument.'[9]

In view of this it is possible to be sympathetic to Tennant's claim: 'Presumably the world is comparable with a single throw of dice. And common sense is not foolish in suspecting the dice to have been loaded.'[10] The reasoning behind this utterance is that although there can be no question of a mathematical probability of the dice's being loaded, the loading is 'alogically' probable. The alogical is said to be 'non-rational, yet reasonable, certitude determined psychologically' and the 'ultimate basis of all scientific induction'; 'in making transition from the probability (relatively to the induction-postulates) of laws, etc., to the probability of the postulates themselves, we are exchanging one meaning of 'probability' – the logical – for another – the psychological'.[11] The implication then is that the postulate of a cosmic teleology should be regarded as epistemologically similar to the postulate of the uniformity of nature. The claim is also made that belief in cosmic teleology is epistemologically similar to belief in the existence of fellow-men.[12] Now both these claims are hollow; the latter because belief in the existence of fellow-men is for us inescapable in a way that belief in cosmic teleology is not (and nor is the existence of God, which undermines the claim made not infrequently that belief in the existence of an external world and belief in the existence of God, or experience of an external world and experience of God, are epistemological equals); the former partly because the future uniformity of nature is not a *postulate*, given belief in the continued existence of the world – and if belief in the continued existence of the world is questioned, then recourse must be had to a cosmological rather than a teleological approach; partly because past uniformity cannot be seriously questioned, whereas in the case of cosmic teleology there is no corresponding unquestioned fact or set of facts capable of playing a corresponding epistemological role – alternatively expressed, we enjoy (virtually) absolute certainty about past uniformity but not about, let us say, the problematic nature of the supposed *explicanda* in cosmic teleology. Thus the analogies drawn are unsatisfactory and Tennant's case makes no progress. On the other hand he is correct in arguing that the singularity of the cosmos does not of itself proscribe cosmic teleology as a plausible hypothesis.

Advocates of cosmic teleology imply that, without recourse to God, if the cosmos were more of a chaos they would be less puzzled, and that if *per impossibile* they could be faced with total chaos their intellectual satisfaction would be complete. In rare cases such as panpsychism this line of thought is plausible – hence the importance of Whitehead's metaphysical account of the cosmos in process natural theology. In other cases, in particular if the world is interpreted as an organic cosmic whole – a view apparently harmonious with both common sense and modern science – the line of thought is totally erroneous. As long as the cosmos is as comparable with a vegetable or atom as with a product of design there is no justification for accepting a cosmic teleological argument.

Moreover it should be emphasised that the foregoing objections equally decisively prohibit consideration of the degree of order in the cosmos from functioning as the basis of a sound cosmic teleological argument, even if it is developed into consideration of this degree of order as the condition of further specific features of the cosmos such as life, mind, consciousness, rationality, personality, moral goodness, beauty. All these features may be proper objects of wonder – and it is a proper function of arguments like Tennant's to show this, to show that in a sense of 'ought' defined by the force of the arguments they ought to occasion wonder (or indeed awe) – but they are not proper causes of intellectual puzzlement. In that sense they are mysteries but not problems; thought-provoking but not perplexing; bewitching but not bemusing.

Failure to draw these last distinctions vitiates Hick's proposal in his *Arguments for the Existence of God* that 'what the teleological argument . . . does is not to establish divine existence, but to pose a question which either has no answer or has God as its answer'. It is possible to concur with the sentiment, 'Cosmic evolution constitutes a transcendence-suggesting mystery to which religion is a natural response', but not with the further contention, 'If this complex evolving cosmos does indeed embody a purpose, then its mystery is illumined by that fact; otherwise it presents a problem that has no solution.'[13] Not so; for otherwise it should not be considered a problem genuinely calling for solution.

The conclusion must be maintained that there is no acceptable independent Qualitative argument for the existence of God. Yet the features of the world which figure prominently in such arguments have a rightful place in any attempted justification of theism. It has already been observed that they operate significantly in a sound subsidiary or dependent argument designed to show that a comparatively characterless CEB posited on other grounds, such as of explanatory ultimacy in connection with contingency, is qualitatively 'this' rather than 'that'. The manner of this operation should now be indicated further.

Introduction of a CEB transforms what have hitherto not been genuine problems into problems by licensing the interpretation of mysteries as puzzles, thereby admitting them as significant evidence. For the introduction of a CEB raises questions about his nature and his purpose in creating the world which can be answered only by moulding the notions of his character and purpose to fit what we know of the world, or, to use I. T. Ramsey's useful little term, by tailoring an 'empirical fit'. And the procedure for achieving such empirical fit is to ask and to answer questions like: Supposing there is a CEB, why is it that the world has the degree of order that it has? Why is it such as to produce life (mind, personality, etc.)? Why is it such as to cause personality to react to it in aesthetic admiration of at times overwhelming intensity? These questions differ from cosmic teleological questions by operating within a context of provisional acceptance of a CEB which prevents them from being 'silly'. They focus on transcendence-suggesting mysteries as indications of the character of a transcendent being rather than that such a being exists – though the former need not exclude the latter, as remains to be seen. Final judgement as to his character depends on judicious assessment of the relevant mysteries and their relevant merits in rival interpretations, for example the problem of evil in the context of a good CEB, the problem of good (covering various features such as meaningfulness, moral achievement, beauty, religious experience) in the context of an evil CEB. (Both problems, let it be repeated, being genuine problems only in the context of provisional acceptance of a CEB.) 'Hard' knockdown arguments play little or no part in such assessment; once again it is necessary to resort to 'soft' (but firm) reasoning. In this connection the kind of reasoning so well illustrated in many of J. Wisdom's writings is most pertinent. Wisdom's work is indeed of considerable value in relation to the justification of theism but apropos of empirical fit only, not as claimed by Hick (and more recently by J. Richmond and B. Mitchell) in the primary stage of justification also; for it is apparently unable in the primary stage of justification to fulfil the crucial function of combating the unrelenting claims of Occam's razor.[14]

A main role then of qualitative features of the world is to function in arguments designed to show that a putative CEB is God rather than Devil or vice versa.

Now whatever judgement is reached about the nature of the CEB, the relation of the argument from contingency to these subsidiary Qualitative arguments may be expressed by saying that it licenses the analogy between the world and a product of (benevolent or malevolent) design being given precedence over the analogy between the world and a vegetable. Yet earlier – the tacit assumption, here retained, being that, as argued in the previous chapter, a theory of benevolent design is preferable to one of malevolent design – it was observed that if such precedence is allowed, there is some force in the cosmic teleological argument as an argument for the *existence* of God, not merely, as in the foregoing account, as an argument for the existence of *God* rather than Devil. It follows that paradoxically there is a certain independent support for an argument from contingency to a CEB or indeed God in a dependent cosmic teleological argument. In non-paradoxical terms, provisional acceptance of the Existential argument from contingency to a CEB (or of this plus Qualitative arguments to the effect that the CEB may be identified with God), by licensing the subordination of the analogy between the cosmos and a vegetable or atom to that between the cosmos and a product of design – and also, it may be added, by providing an explanatory ultimate – removes the two significant, indeed decisive, obstacles to a cosmic teleological argument, and allows the relevant features of the world to function as evidence in Qualitative arguments which genuinely support (and oppose) the conclusion of the Existential argument. Thus empirical fit may function in at least two ways, one 'concept-developmental', the other 'confirmatory'. To the extent that 'dependent teleological questions' (as they may be called) of the kind instanced above in connection with empirical fit receive plausible and satisfying answers in terms of the hypothesis of a CEB or of God, to that extent does the hypothesis receive confirmation. Thus, as Ramsey himself makes plain, empirical fit fills for metaphysical hypotheses the role filled by experimental verification/falsification for scientific hypotheses.[15]

There is a further way, however, in which empirical fit may function. For even though there are reasons for not pressing the analogy, reasons which preclude its being taken as a genuine problem to be solved in an independent Qualitative argument, the very fact that the world permits comparison with a product of design supports to some extent the view that it is such a product – compare the negative effect that the impossibility of such an analogy would have. (The possibility of significantly pressing tensed cosmic teleological questions is also relevant here.) Moreover this is logically quite independent of any argument from contingency or of provisional acceptance of such an argument. Thus although in isolation it is of little or no significance, in conjunction with another argument such as the argument from contingency its value is by no means negligible; for by virtue of its logical independence it is able to act as confirmation of such an argument *in addition* to the confirmation provided by dependent Qualitative arguments, even though the qualitative features taken as evidence (order, beauty, etc.) may be identical in both cases and may indeed function additionally in concept-developmental Qualitative arguments. This third function of empirical fit is 'confirmatory' too, then, but needs to be distinguished from the second. It is useful to speak of 'loose empirical fit' in this function and of 'tight empirical fit' in the second. These labels indicate the greater measure of support provided in the second function, not least because there, as is not the case in the third function, there is good reason to press the analogy and work out its implications.

It should perhaps be pointed out that the use of Qualitative arguments in making out claims to loose empirical fit is not exposed to the following criticism: 'One occasionally hears teachers of theology aver that although the proofs do not provide conclusive grounds for belief in God, they are at least pointers, indicators. But a fallacious argument points nowhere (except to the lack of logical acumen on the part of those who accept it).'[16] The point about cosmic teleological arguments is that although they are unacceptable as isolated independent justification, they are not totally fallacious.

The conclusion stands then that Qualitative arguments may play a threefold role in the justification of theism. Firstly there is the possibility of a concept-developmental role, filling out the character of a CEB posited on other grounds, acting as arguments for God rather than Devil. Secondly there is the confirmatory role, where the actual positing of a CEB or God is supported by qualitative considerations. In both cases Qualitative arguments are necessarily dependent on an Existential argument which remains the linchpin in any justification of theism. Finally there is the independent confirmatory role, where the evidential value of qualitative features does not presuppose provisional acceptance of the theistic (or quasi-theistic) hypothesis. Thus the traditional influence of Qualitative arguments is after all seen to be in no way completely unwarranted.

The practical application of these conclusions, as also further consideration of their position in the overall pattern of justification, will be pursued later.

7 Christian Theism: Some Problems of Definition and Methodology

Part of the argument of the preceding chapters was in support of identifying the CEB not only with the God of religion but with the Christian God. Yet the manner of this identification had implications about the nature of Christianity, for example with regard to miracles, the incarnation, the atonement, the trinity and the nature of God, which would be rejected by many or indeed most Christians. The question must therefore be raised whether the position outlined there deserves the label 'Christian'.

Yet since there is no single agreed definition of 'Christian' the question is not a simple one to answer. Even if it should be agreed that what is fundamental is the living faith of the church rather than divisive beliefs, clearly there are limits somewhere as to what may properly be counted as 'Christian' beliefs. R. B. Braithwaite and P. van Buren, for example, have rightly been almost universally charged with transgressing those limits. Yet the views advanced here are nothing like so controversial as theirs, and without engaging in detailed discussion as to the location of the limits of minimal Christian belief it may justifiably be claimed that a position composed of the following views is within the fold.

1. A transcendent, loving, creator (and in that sense omnipotent) God exists.
2. He has revealed himself.
3. He has revealed himself as a God of redemptive love.
4. The focal point of this revelation is found in Jesus.
5. He is active in ('in') the world.
6. He may be and is apprehended by ordinary folk.

Further, it would appear plausible to add as entirely consonant with, and in some measure implicit in, the position developed previously:

7. He is distinctively active in the lived faith of the community of the church.
8. The church is the community of religious responders to the focal revelation of God in Jesus.

Such a combination of views is less than full-blown orthodoxy but is without difficulty recognisably Christian.

This conclusion holds even though, as must now be made explicit, the concept of deity sustained by the soft argument from contingency is that of a temporal deity. Creativity as interpreted in the argument is correlative with temporality. On the other hand they are emphatically not interchangeable. Creativity is temporal but temporality is not of itself creative; nor is temporal change creative in the radical sense in which 'creativity' is being used here, despite the fact that in the course of temporal change qualitative novelty may arise. If they were we could say of the temporal cosmos itself that it is self-creating. To some this may appear an attractive view, and it can be a useful metaphor, but it is shallow metaphysics. For within our personal experience we distinguish between merely existing or changing temporally and actually *creating*. Creativity is thus qualitatively different, and it is in virtue of this difference that the concept can be used explanatorily, that the CEB is a cosmos-*explaining*-being, and that a self-creating CEB is to a large extent a self-explanatory being. It may be seen by contrast moreover that matter pursuing its course, even if productive of qualitative novelty, is not self-creating and not self-explanatory.

The objection will be lodged that a temporal deity is a (mere) finite God, a petty entity compared with the majesty of the timeless infinite deity worshipped down the ages in the mainstream of the Christian tradition. Yet the objection suffers from the gravest of difficulties. In the first place it is arguable that the notion of a timeless deity has played a comparatively minor role in the actual worship of the majority of believers, whatever may have been true of the handful of scholared ecclesiastical intellectuals. Secondly and consequently, the notion of a temporal deity cannot easily be dismissed as religiously unsatisfying.

Thirdly, a doctrine of such notorious obscurity as that of a time-less God requires very strong supporting reasons in order to be allowed to maintain its place, and these are conspicuously lack-ing. It is said for example that a temporal form of existence is inherently limited in a way that timeless existence is not; but when pressed, this objection seems to rest on the illicit inference that because human selves are both temporal and limited, any temporal self must be subject to similar reprehensible limi-tations. In fact our limitations may not be at all inherent in tem-porality – thus, for example, a temporal deity might well be troubled neither by faulty memory nor by an inability to foresee the general trend of things; that is to say, he might be 'omnis-cient' in the sense of knowing all that it could be open to anyone to know. Moreover any deity must be limited to some extent by virtue of being himself and no other entity. Consequently it cuts little ice to make the following kind of charge: 'If God were tem-poral . . . his present . . . would be limited by his past and fu-ture.' Similarly weak is the further argument that 'the fact that we need to act with reference to our fixed past and our uncer-tain future restricts the nature of our willing', and that unless God were timeless he would be correspondingly imperfect.[1]

More serious if it could be maintained is the contention that if God were temporal his existence would be contingent and no explanation of the world's existence; but this objection is fully met by the soft argument from contingency which firmly rebuts the view that 'if God is a necessary being he must exist in a time-less present'.[2]

A further objection is that divine temporality contradicts di-vine transcendence. Yet this presupposes a fixed and agreed notion of transcendence, whereas as in the case of 'Christian' there is scope for legitimate disagreement. As will be apparent by the end of this chapter, 'transcendence' may be understood in a way that does not exclude temporality.

Mascall insists that 'the act in which God both preserves and knows the finite universe must necessarily be timeless and spaceless, since its object is the totality of spatio-temporal exist-ence'.[3] Yet it is not claimed here that the object of any actual act of God includes the totality of temporal existence (tenseless) as Mascall's argument requires.

According to H. Meynell, 'if God exists and is in the proper sense omniscient, then either determinism is inevitable, or God's knowledge must be conceived as outside time'.[4] The course taken here is to deny determinism and affirm divine temporality while conceding that God is not in the 'proper' sense omniscient, that is, he does not have complete knowledge of the future. Yet this is not estimated an unworthy attribute of deity.

It is possible that if the notion of a timeless deity can be defended as coherent – a further very considerable difficulty in objections to temporal theism – it is a concept of deity superior to that of a temporal deity. This is the main thrust of Owen's argument, and the considerations advanced here do not amount to its rebuttal. Yet it would be methodologically improper to infer from this conclusion, if it should prove acceptable, that the concept of a temporal deity is so inferior as not to be worthy of serious attention, either intellectual or religious; moreover such an inference is equally improper if made regarding concepts of deity 'finite' in other respects. The point at stake here has been so admirably expressed by P. C. Appleby that his conclusion must be quoted.

Appleby sets out to oppose the kind of view exemplified in J. N. Findlay's remark that it is 'wholly anomalous to worship anything *limited* in any thinkable manner. For all limited superiorities are tainted with an obvious relativity, and can be dwarfed in thought by still mightier superiorities, in which process of being dwarfed they lose their claim upon our worshipful attitudes.'[5] Appleby has little difficulty in showing that religious attitudes, including that of worship, are considerably more flexible than this. The obvious and decisive point here is that in any contest of worship-value a Findlayan ideal deity, if it remain but an ideal, must be beaten hands down by an otherwise inferior but actual deity. What matters is which exists, not which is abstractly ideal. (This judgement is of course by no means completely beyond question, but it recommends itself to 'common sense' and receives further attention later.) The conclusion correctly drawn by Appleby is that 'the criteria of adequacy for objects of worship, such as they are, do in fact define a limited range of religiously acceptable deities, but one which is much broader than many philosophers have realised it to be'. In particular,

if a reasonably intelligent and well-informed inhabitant of a modern civilisation were tempted to worship anything, he would require a deity of great power, knowledge and goodness, one who is not subject to the usual vicissitudes of time, and one who is capable of personal communication with humans. These considerations rule out gods who are feeble, stupid or malevolent, and the ineffable Absolutes of many metaphysical systems. But they leave open a broad range between the outer limits of immanence and transcendence, a range which cannot be further restricted by analysis of religious attitudes alone. The conflicts between finitist and traditional theologies . . . will have to be resolved on other grounds. And so will the question whether there are in fact any appropriate objects of the attitudes of worship.[6]

To this it is necessary only to add that the grounds for deciding whether any appropriate object of worship exists, and the grounds for resolving the conflicts between finitist and traditional theologies, will in large measure coincide. The basic move from which all else follows must be to decide which concept of deity is called for, and justified as instantiated, by the facts and by considerations of coherence. The extent to which such a deity is religiously acceptable (or Christianly acceptable or whatever) will then be apparent, as will its position on the finitist–traditional spectrum.

The starting-point of this procedure needs a little elaboration. It is methodologically unsound to begin with a fixed concept of deity and then inquire what evidence there is that such a being exists (evidence which, as has been emphasised, must centre on *explicanda*). Yet it would be unrealistic to urge that one should begin only with the problem to be solved, and allow one's concept of the *explicans* to be wholly determined by it alone. It cannot be done, partly because of the prevalence of ideas of God, partly because the relevance of evidence is conditioned by ideas of God. The most acceptable procedure is to entertain initially a relatively indeterminate concept (as in the soft argument from contingency) which may then be trimmed according to the supporting evidence which in turn is thereby accorded due prominence. In this way there is a prospect of overcoming unwarranted though sometimes unquestioned presuppositions, and of countering the enormous weight of history behind doctrinal errors which, as Hartshorne has neatly observed, 'are beloved along with the truth in the seemingly unitary beauty of the great traditions'.[7]

If the assessment of evidence in this study is basically correct, the only firm starting-point for the justification of theism lies in contingency, from which may be developed a soft argument from contingency culminating in a temporal deity. Consequently either this deity is accepted by Christians, or it is rejected and Christian theism stands bereft of intellectual justification. Reasons were given for relating this deity intimately with Jesus, and for interpreting the CEB in broadly Christian terms. The temporality of the deity is no reason for revising this judgement.

On the contrary; in hitherto perhaps the most careful systematic exploration of the theme of timelessness in Christian theism, N. Pike concludes:

> my opinion is considerably more negative than I had anticipated it would be at the outset. . . . It is now my suspicion that the doctrine of God's timelessness was introduced into Christian theology because Platonic thought was stylish at the time and because the doctrine appeared to have considerable advantage from the point of view of systematic elegance. . . . Once introduced, it took on a life of its own. [Regarding the supposed systematic elegance, however,] the evidence I have been able to uncover . . . seems to pull rather firmly toward the opposite view. [Moreover] there appears to be little reason to think that this doctrine is implied by the basic Christian concept of God . . . , nor have I been able to find any basis for it in biblical literature or in the confessional literature of either the Catholic or Protestant Churches.

Rather does the evidence again point rather clearly in the other direction.[8] Pike refrains from going so far as to claim that the doctrine of timelessness should be excluded from Christian theology; but that further step is taken here on grounds which lie outside the scope of his study, namely on grounds arising from consideration of the possibility and nature of the justification of theism.

A natural corollary of the views developed hitherto is that the God in whom it may be justifiable to believe is a changing deity;

this is suggested by his initiative, responsiveness and temporality. Similar objections and counter-objections may be made in this case as in that of temporality. Surely the essential point is that, provided the change is not out of character, it presents no problem – a point repeatedly and powerfully pressed by Hartshorne. 'He who refuses to rejoice with the joy of others is as selfish as he who refuses to grieve with their sorrows.' 'We do not admire a man less because we know he would be a happier man if his son, who is wretched, became well and happy, or because we anticipate that when a child is born to him it will enrich his life with many new joys.' The parallels are clear, and taking the argument to its logical conclusion Hartshorne sensibly claims that 'the higher the being the more dependence of certain kinds will be appropriate for it'. In this sense (only) it is possible to agree with Whitehead's much-reviled dictum: 'It is as true to say that God creates the World, as that the *World* creates *God*.'[9]

It should not be thought, however, that the concept of deity adumbrated here is identical with a process theological one, particularly as represented by Hartshorne. Although there are similarities, in his work there is an emphasis on divine perfection which is not a necessary part of the concept developed here. For him too God is necessarily a creator, 'incapable of not creating, though perfectly capable of not creating this or that creature – any creature you choose'. In that sense he is necessarily dependent on *some world or other*, a view not adopted here. Again, Hartshorne insists that 'God literally contains the universe', he is 'literally all-inclusive'.[10] This is the celebrated doctrine of panentheism – God is both the cosmos and something independent of it, both the Many (by virtue of literally containing the universe of actual entities) and the One (by virtue of being the all-inclusive entity). Yet in the first place it is impossible to take 'literally' literally, in view of God's non-spatiality and cosmic transcendence (which Hartshorne does not deny). Secondly, the analogy between the divine Self and human selves militates against the doctrine – we do not 'contain' each other. Thirdly and decisively, nothing in the argument developed here even suggests, let alone justifies, such a doctrine. On the contrary, the essence of the argument lies in contrasting cosmic contingent existence with divine necessary or ontologically independent existence, and each of these logically excludes the other as a mode of existence of one and the same being. This is not to deny that there may be contingencies or accidents in the divine nature, as there must be if God is temporal, responsive and changing, but it is to deny that his action in continuing his existence is in any way dependent on something 'outside' him as the continued existence of the cosmos is dependent on his sustaining activity.

The logical contradiction in Hartshorne's position here is not avoided by referring God's necessity and his (ontological) contingency to different 'aspects' of his nature, the former to what elsewhere is termed his 'abstract identity' and the latter to his 'concrete existence'.[11] In the first place, just what is meant by 'abstract identity'? Secondly, what is the ontological relation between the two aspects? From the meaning of 'ontological independence' it should follow that his 'abstract identity' is divorced from his 'concrete existence', which is doubtless a further contribution to the Many, but what price the One?

There is no way forward here, and fortunately no real need to try. According to Hartshorne in *The Divine Relativity* (though not elsewhere) 'there are logically the three views: (1) God is merely the cosmos, in all aspects inseparable from the sum or system of dependent things or effects; (2) he is both this system and something independent of it; (3) he is not the system, but is in all aspects independent'.[12] Wishing to avoid the third of these without lapsing into pantheism, the first, Hartshorne plumps for the second. Yet of course these three do not exhaust the possibilities. On the view adopted here, God is distinct from the system and yet in some ways dependent on it, not ontologically, but affected by it. Hartshorne equates panentheism and sur-relativism (his doctrine that God is eminently or supremely relative), but this is unnecessary.

Hartshorne also labels his view 'dipolar' theism in opposition to the 'monopolar' tradition of classical theism. What is meant by this is reasonably clear from the foregoing. God exists not only in unity but also in multiplicity. Again, he is not only cause and active but also, by virtue of the world's action on him, effect and passive. He is by nature necessary (in a sense which is said to permit the ontological argument to work) yet also contingent. He is independent but also dependent. Absolute yet relative. Eternal in the sense of ungenerated yet temporal. Now there are ways of reconciling some of these apparent contradictories (eternal and temporal, independent and dependent, cause and effect, necessary and contingent) without positing a dual-aspect theism or landing in self-contradiction. To this extent the dipolar approach has much to recommend it. It is healthy that the monopolar monopoly be called in question even if not overthrown, and here perhaps lies the main positive contribution of process theology. Although ample reason may be found for rejecting process thought as the basis of a natural theology, its quickening of reflection on concepts of deity is a notable and welcome achievement. On the other hand, as an exercise, albeit unintentional, in ontological dismembering of the Godhead, dipolarity is intellectually invidious.

Finally, a word on the finite–infinite polarity. 'A finite God' is more often than not a term of denigration, and more often than not unjustifiably so. For if 'infinite' is interpreted as 'not finite', then since there are a number of ways of being finite it remains virtually vacuous until cashed by specifying 'not finite in this way, in that way, in such and such a way . . .'. Yet defenders of a so-called 'finite' God also insist that he is 'not finite in this way, in that way, in such and such a way . . .'. Now they will clearly differ in their specifications from defenders of a so-called 'infinite' God, yet there will be some overlap, perhaps considerable; from which it is apparent that in this interpretation the finite–infinite dichotomy is crude and misleading. Other important interpretations of 'infinite' as applied to God are 'not limited by other self-subsistents' and 'perfect'.[13] The former applies specifically to the deity defended here; the latter may well do so too, and even if not, the failure does not necessarily signal lack of religious worth as an object of worship, in which case 'finite' as a derogatory label begs the basic question. Again the finite–infinite dichotomy is misleading. It might indeed with profit be abandoned altogether.

The methodological proposal that one should begin with a relatively indeterminate concept of deity and with *explicanda*, and proceed only so far as the evidence and considerations of coherence warrant, is relevant in answering a further possible objection, namely that the doctrines, explicit and implicit, presented here as the emaciated survivors (so it will seem to many) of the full-blooded corpus of living truth nurtured by the church down the centuries can be of little or no value in responding to man's needs. For if doctrines, which from the point of view of their content are relevant to man's needs, lack warrant of their truth, they are or rationally should be impotent to minister to those needs. Conversely, if doctrines have some warrant of truth, albeit being at first sight at least less relevant to man's needs from the point of view of their content, they may in the long run prove infinitely more valuable in ministering to perhaps fewer but very real needs. And of course in some cases, as was intimated earlier with regard to traditional Christian doctrines of atonement and incarnation, it may be that what appeared to be needs are not needs at all.

Yet it must be conceded that if allegedly religious doctrines evolved as here in a philosophical context do not in fact meet real needs, they are not truly religious. For it appears to be a necessary condition of religious truth that it mediate help of some sort. ('The Ideal, the Need, the Deliverer – these are the three objects which the individual experience, as a source of religious insight, has always undertaken to reveal.'[14] On the other hand the 'emaciated' Christianity presented here seems to fulfil this condition with its doctrines of divine action, revelation, redemptive love, and personal relationships with individuals.

In conclusion it is worth listing the features of deity which have emerged from or are implicit in the argument defended in the present study, along with brief mention of the reasons for holding to them:

1. Non-material	This is a *sine qua non* of an explanation of the whole physical cosmos (along with its pockets of non-materiality).
2. One	This follows from the principle of parsimony.
3. Self	The natural analogy to develop, increasingly justified by its fruitfulness.
4. Creator-sustainer	The natural development of the basic analogy, illuminating the sense of contingency and coping

	in part with world-contingency questions. Refers to God's activity '*on*' the world rather than '*in*' it (9 below).
5. Self-creator	A natural, consistent, explanatory extension of the basic analogy enabling it to cope completely with world-contingency questions (other than 'silly' ones).
	Other terms which might be used here are self-existent, self-caused, ontologically self-sufficient, self-explanatory, ontologically independent, first cause, factually necessary.
6. (*a*) Good	An attribute justified by our estimation of the cosmos.
(*b*) Perfect	A not unjustified though rather indirect speculative extension of (*a*).
(*c*) Incorruptible	This follows from 5 and 6(*b*) and is conditional on acceptance of the latter.
7. Temporal-eternal	Follows from the nature of the soft argument from contingency.
8. Indestructible (externally)	This follows from 4 and 5. It is not the case that God happens never to be destroyed; rather is it that there are no powers capable of destroying him, except himself.
9. Active in the world (*a*) In religious experience (*b*) In revelation	A plausible interpretation, on the basis of other characteristics of the CEB, of contingency experiences, of religious experiences, and of revelation.
10. Changing	A plausible inference from 6, 7 and 9.
11. Omnipresent	This follows from 4. N. Smart speaks more accurately of 'secret omnipresence'.

12. Omnipotent	This follows from 4 and 5, but needs to be interpreted in such a way that it is consonant with, for example, divine inability to be the direct and sole agent of the free and responsible actions of non-divine beings.
13. Conscious	This chimes in naturally with all the others and follows in particular from 6 and 9.
14. Supremely knowledgeable	This follows from 4, 5, 12 and 13, plus the plausible supposition that the supreme being is not forgetful; but it is not intended to include complete knowledge of the future.
15. Passible	A special form of 10, though traditionally discussed separately. It is irresistibly suggested by 6, 7, 9, 10, 13 and 14.

There remain to be mentioned the concepts of transcendence and immanence.

Either 9 alone or the combination of 9, 4 and 11 may be said to define divine immanence. If emphasis is placed on the contrast between 4 and 9, the latter alone signifies immanence (11 being tied to 4). Yet since the former represents the opposite of that aloof separation which is one kind of transcendence, it may be taken along with 11 as a form of immanence complementing 9.

The combinations either of, 1, 4, 5 and 11 or of 1, 4, 5, 9 and 11 may be said to define divine transcendence. In the former case, 4 is interpreted as contrasting with 9 which is therefore excluded as being a form of immanence. In the latter, 9 is interpreted as a complementary form of transcendence on the ground that the mode of divine action referred to transcends, as does all divine action, any of which an account is in principle possible within a naturalistic framework.

None of the preceding four possibilities can be equated

with each other. The plea may therefore be added that transcendence and immanence never be so interpreted that they are equivalent. It is not fruitful to urge: ' "within" is an analogy like "beyond" – not to be taken literally: who is to say that "within" and "beyond" point in different directions?'[15]

The fifteen elements listed above coalesce to form what is still to some extent an indeterminate and indeed an untraditional concept of deity. Yet perhaps the loss of certain traditional elements has compensations in the form of gains in intelligibility and coherence. And relative indeterminacy is a healthy sign in any concept of God in view of the gulf by which we are separated from him.

8 Problems of Reference and Analogy

Ideally I would include at this point a further defence of the concept of deity which has emerged, to the effect that its degree of coherence and intelligibility is such as to shield it from the criticism that theism is factually meaningless, that 'God exists' makes no significant truth-claim, being neither true nor false but nonsensical. However, I have argued elsewhere that it is possible to make a reasonably adequate reference to a transcendent God as logical subject, and must here refer the reader to that source.[1] There too I presuppose that divine transcendence may be hospitable to temporality. Certainly the inclusion of temporality and change in the concept of God facilitates, and may even save the possibility of, an intelligible individuating description of him.

Clearly, however, of pivotal importance in such defence of theism as has been given above and as is given in 'Referring to God' is the analogical extension of key words beyond their normal usage. Initially the need was discovered even in a naturalistic context for prising 'in' out of a rigid empirical setting and placing it in a looser framework. Capitalising on this move, terms like 'self', 'creative', 'cause' and 'beyond', as well as 'in', were used in a non-naturalistic context. The justification for this is that such terms seem to lend themselves to semantic extension without leading to incoherence. If this be so, it implies a theory of loose or fluid meaning, with a penumbra of meaning surrounding (certain) terms outside the limits set by a literal-minded empiricism or naturalism, yet within the limits set by self-contradiction and undeniable vacuity. The possibility of such a theory is in any event suggested by the prevalence of fluid meaning in a naturalistic context, not only in a contentious case like 'in' but in cases like 'religion', 'Christian', 'person', the names of colours in transitional areas on a spectrum, or any case where there are problems of definition. These problems suggest that it is not open to a literal-minded empiricism or naturalism to eliminate penumbrae of meaning, except arbitrarily; and if they are not eliminated who is to say, without begging basic questions, that they cannot extend to cover non-naturalistic particulars and events? Thus the literal–analogical contrast should be held to operate in the context of semantic continua covering both secular and religious usage, rather than with neat secular semantic containers and rather less neat if not downright grubby religious semantic containers. Or we might say that the move from logical atomism to family resemblances should not be restricted to networks of naturalistic meaning.

Scope for endless disagreement is apparent here. The extent to which a theistic account is deemed satisfactory depends on how close key terms are held to approach the pole of vacuity, and for settling this there are no clear-cut criteria. Understanding permits of degrees. However, the greater number of non-analogical elements included by theists in their concept of God, such as temporality, passibility and change, the less serious the problem. (That is to say, non-analogical *secular* elements. As N. Smart has observed, there are non-analogical *religious* terms, i.e. terms used literally in religion and analogically in other spheres; for example 'holy', and even 'God'. The point about the latter, however, is that it has to be cashed in terms taken from secular usage, with attendant problems of factual intelligibility.[2])

No proper emphasis on fluid meaning can license the extension of concepts without due care, but it is a useful weapon for opposing claims that all basic theistic assertions are factually meaningless. The texture of language is softer than many a linguistic tailor suspects, and capable of taking on more shapes than exist in the pattern-books of the more severely and restrictedly empiricist.

How is this related to traditional theories of analogy? It suggests a more 'radical' approach, that is to say, one that gets to the roots of the problem; for the traditional theories of analogy of attribution and analogy of proportionality are insufficiently comprehensive. According to the analogy of attribution God is good because he causes goodness, personal because he causes personality, and so on. But quite apart from difficulties raised by this, such as whether there must be any real likeness between cause and effect, the rock-bottom objection is this: 'cause' is here necessarily used to operate the analogy of attribution; but it is used in a sense different from its intramundane use, that is, it is used analogically; yet this analogical use cannot itself be interpreted in terms of analogy of attribution because it is presupposed by it. Thus analogy of attribution is insufficiently comprehensive.

Nor can this fault be remedied by using analogy of proportionality to get it started, since what analogy of proportionality asserts is that there is a relational likeness between the way in which (some) human attributes are proportioned to human nature and the way in which God's attributes are proportioned to his nature; it refrains from direct comparison of human and divine attributes. It is thus uninformative unless we have some antecedent knowledge of God's nature and attributes; but such knowledge could self-evidently not be interpreted in terms of analogy of proportionality for it would be presupposed by it. Thus analogy of proportionality is also revealed as insufficiently comprehensive. Neither individually nor jointly do these two theories reach the root of the problem.

Owen attempts to avoid this conclusion by allowing antecedent knowledge of God's nature which is literal and hence permits analogy of proportionality to get started without leaving a residue of unexplained analogical usage. 'God is not entirely unknown before the application of predicates; he is defined as self-existent being; and this definition determines the predicated reference.'[3] However, we saw in connection with Owen's defence of the cosmological argument that his 'self-existent being' is at best a logical stop-card bearing no apprehensible markings, and at worst incoherent; and even the former alternative does not lend itself to a very informative use of analogy of proportionality. Yet quite apart from this the fact remains, as Owen insists, that analogy of proportionality must depend on analogy of attribution if it is not to be uninformative since it refrains from direct comparison of human and divine attributes, and there seems to be no way of even beginning to repair the basic defect of the latter.

This defect is treated as less than basic by Owen, as also by

Mascall, both of whom argue that analogy of attribution and analogy of proportionality are jointly sufficient. Thus according to Owen 'the analogy of attribution tells us that God is the cause of all finite properties' and 'the fact of creation is . . . the basis of analogical predication'.[4] Yet although he asserts that 'God's creative act is not an instance of general causality', he sees no difficulty in our being able to 'grasp' the unique fact of creation and then proceed by analogy of attribution, whereas in fact the nature of the understanding of the key analogical terms, 'creation', or 'cause', used to describe the unique fact grasped, itself requires interpretation in terms of a theory of analogy. Mascall is exposed to similar criticism when he urges that 'the first cause and the creature are directly related by the relation of creation, which thus, as it were, cuts horizontally across the analogy of proportionality with an analogy of attribution'.[5]

The different approach suggested by the soft argument from contingency and subsequent discussion is some kind of 'model' theory, as suggested notably by I. T. Ramsey. The key model is of course 'self', which is then qualified in various ways – 'cosmic', 'supreme', 'cosmos-creating', 'self-creating'. Such a theory does not presuppose any analogical use of language to refer to God which eludes interpretation in terms of the theory itself, and thus it gets to the root of the problem in a way that traditional theories do not.

On the other hand the model theory implied by the present study differs from Ramsey's at two points at least.

Firstly, greater descriptive force is attributed to qualifiers. For him they act as directives or imperatives rather than descriptives, telling us to develop a (descriptive) model in a particular way until a disclosure occurs and we 'see' the (largely or partly) indescribable mystery of God.[6] However, 'self-creating' for example appears to be, and is intended to be, descriptive. Perhaps then it is not properly a qualifier? Perhaps we should take 'self-creator' as a model? But this is impossible, for the characteristic of a model is that it is 'something about which we are reasonably clear by which to understand something which is very problematical' – and the notion of self-creation is more problematical than pellucid. Again, 'beyond' is intended to be descriptive rather than imperative.[7] There would seem to be room then for descriptive qualifiers (in a somewhat indefinite sense of 'descriptive' which takes full account of the penumbrae of analogical meaning and the essential elusiveness of the divine mystery) as well as imperatives. Perhaps Ramsey does not intend the qualifiers to lack all descriptive force; but even if not, there is a difference of emphasis here.

Secondly and crucially, although there is a significant role for some kind of disclosure in the present theory (since in the end one simply 'sees' the point or meaning of various identifying references – the penny has to drop), it concerns the meaning of key terms only; it does not include as for Ramsey their 'inalienable reference'. Although Ramsey is a *qualified* intuitionist – the models generating and generated by disclosures have to display empirical fit – he is an intuitionist in his insistence on the cognitive nature of all disclosures, his insistence that all disclosures have objective reference, and in his attempt to make them do the work traditionally done by the 'proofs' of natural theology ('all the traditional proofs of God's existence can be regarded, in principle, as techniques to evoke disclosures'); thus although models used to describe the referent may be corrigible, their referent itself is guaranteed.[8] In the present theory not even the *meaning* of key terms is *guaranteed* by the penny dropping (it may rise again); their referent most certainly is not – hence the need for something like the soft argument from contingency in addition (it may be) to putative disclosures.

Finally, it may be mentioned that in the present account the emphasis on the 'self' model is if anything even firmer than Ramsey's. This is curious when one reflects that he has repeatedly and illuminatingly expounded the supra-empirical element in human nature and then moved on to speak of the cosmos as empirical *and more* in similar vein. Yet at two points at least he suggests the possibility of 'activity' as a super-model for God, integrating both personal and non-personal models. Thus he writes: 'I would not care to speak in the material mode of the "personality of God". Rather would I speak of the possibility of talking in terms of a personal model of that which confronts us *actively* in a cosmic disclosure.' Impersonal models are, however, also in order. Yet there is no conflict between the two kinds since they are not *pic-*

turing models.[9]

Even if the lack of conflict be admitted, this is unsatisfactory. The Christian God at any rate is believed to be essentially personal, not an unknowable mystery better characterised by a personality-neutral super-model than by a personal model. And this view of God is supported by the soft argument from contingency where preference is expressed for the 'self' model rather than any other on account of its superior explanatory power. Moreover it is difficult to see how Ramsey's view can do justice to the concept of revelation; for if revelation does not include essentially personal divine action, it collapses into a purely human experiencing-as, in which case the concept of *revelation* may as well be abandoned.

There is a further difficulty in Ramsey's use of 'activity'. He argues that activity is revealed both in 'cosmic disclosures' and 'self-disclosures', and that the (active) objective constituents of both are linked 'by a concept of activity which carries over *literally* from subject to object'.[10] Now it is impossible to accept this unless it means that the cosmos is revealed as personal, or 'cosmic-self-disclosing'; for if the cosmos is revealed as non-personal the concept of activity cannot carry over '*literally* from [personal] subject to object' – 'personal activity' is not *univocal* with 'non-personal activity'. Yet if this is the meaning, then quite apart from the reprehensible intuitionism involved, the notion of 'activity' as a *super*-model, above the personal–impersonal distinction, is clearly contradicted. The only way to avoid the contradiction is to claim that 'activity' in personal cases is after all univocal with 'activity' in impersonal or non-personal ones – but this is surely unacceptable, cf. 'personal activity' and 'molecular activity'; they are no more univocal than are 'life' as referring to people and 'life' as referring to plants.

In any event, in the view adopted here 'self' is the model *par excellence* in terms of which God is to be understood. No non-personal model can compete with it, and even if it does not 'picture' God it does in a way describe him when suitably qualified. To a certain and important extent then, though by no means sufficiently to call in question his transcendence or worshipfulness, God is less of a mystery than Ramsey's account suggests; and other accounts too. By way of conclusion I would say that God can be described sufficiently to permit a reasonably adequate reference to him, though the description must fall short of being adequate to his nature.

9 The Logic of a Credible Natural Theology

(i) *Criteria of Religious Truth*

We are now in a position to take up the question of criteria of religious truth in general and of theistic truth in particular, and to propose specific criteria. A most impressive and most valuable analysis of the problem has been presented by W. A. Christian, and it is on the basis of a consideration of his views that my own proposals are developed.[1]

Christian suggests criteria for assessing the truth of basic religious proposals. A 'basic religious proposal' is a proposal of the form '*x* is P', where '*x*' expresses the central concept of some doctrinal scheme, like Allah, and 'P' expresses a basic religious predicate like 'holy', 'supreme goal of life', or 'most important'. The criteria offered fall into two parts, the first of which is restricted to four criteria for deciding whether the proposal even makes a significant truth-claim, let alone whether it is true. Christian's summary of all the criteria, introduced as 'some conditions which a complete argument would need to satisfy', is as follows:

> A. It would need to be shown that some basic religious proposal satisfies the conditions of making a significant truth-claim, namely, that it permits of self-consistent formulation, that it permits the formulation of a self-consistent negation so that disagreement is possible, that it permits some reference to its logical subject and that some support of its predication is possible.
>
> B. It would have to be shown that in the circumstances we have sufficient warrant for accepting the proposal (i.e. since it is a proposal for belief, for making an affirmative judgement). This would involve showing:

B1. That in the circumstances (including the general conditions of human life and the consequences of deciding or
failing to decide between the proposal and its alternatives)
the need for decision is sufficiently urgent; and

B2. That our warrant for its truth is sufficiently good,
which would mean that:

(B2*a*) It is possible to make a reasonably successful and
adequate reference to its logical subject, and

(B2*b*) The available principles of judgement are reasonably clear and complete, and

(B2*c*) The available facts give reasonably adequate support for ascribing the predicate to its logical subject.

Thus B1 and B2 condition one another.[2]

Now in my view Christian has established his case for the four
criteria in part A, and I shall not discuss these further. With
regard to B, all should be reasonably clear except (B2*b*). Christian uses 'principles of judgement' to cover three things:

(i) 'Rules of relevance'. These focus the issue to be judged.
They are rules to follow in deciding *what* is (what facts are) relevant to the ascription of a particular predicate. For example, if
the issue under debate is whether a person M is honest, rules of
relevance would be: 'Give particular attention to M's moral
dispositions and conduct'; 'See whether he, habitually, does
not deceive himself or others in what he says and does.'

(ii) 'Norms of judgement'. These tell us *how* to take account
of the relevant facts. For example: 'Trust your own impressions
of M more than N's opinion of M' – or vice versa.[3]

(iii) 'Procedure for judgement'. Christian's discussion of this
is rather scanty; but in trying to decide what it is that is most
important the procedure might be put as follows: 'Compare the
most promising candidate (X) with other promising candidates. Is X more important than Y? Generally speaking, in the
conduct of life does X have to be taken account of more than Y?
Is it such that I have to give it more weight in making decisions,
generally speaking? Continue in this way for all promising candidates. The final issue for judgement is, Is X more important
than everything else?'[4]

Condition B1 is also novel in the present study but its meaning is reasonably clear. It springs from the fact that religious

truth is held to be a matter of existential concern rather than mere speculative interest. Yet the degree of concern varies perhaps depending on the precise nature of a given basic religious proposal, and the warranted response to some might be agnosticism.

So much by way of summary exposition. Moving on to comment, whereas Christian apparently takes 'basic religious proposal' in such a way that something or other must be P (for he presupposes 'basic religious suppositions' of the form 'There is something which is P'), so that the issue turns on which of several possible candidates *x, y* or *z* is P, I wish to allow the possibility that nothing may be P (thus my basic religious supposition is of the form 'There *may be* something which is P'). It is important therefore that the scheme of criteria should cater for arguments to the effect that *x exists* (or 'is real', or 'subsists', to cover ideals, transcendent states, etc., as alternatives to transcendent existents), as well as that *x* is P.

Indeed, the latter may be regarded as a very subsidiary issue. P, as a *basic* religious predicate, is intended to be very general so that adherents of different religions may agree that, whatever is the subject term of a basic religious proposal, any believer in that logical subject could say of it that it was P. Christian suggests 'most important' as P, but 'the proper object/goal of worship and/or contemplation' might be better. Now the point to be noticed here is that with a religious predicate as broad as this, it is analytically true that if the putative referent of the subject term of a basic religious proposal exists (is real, subsists), then the predicate applies to it. It would be a logical contradiction to assert both that the Christian (Jewish, Moslem) God exists and that God is not P; similarly with Nirvana, Brahman, Ahura Mazda, and so on. Thus '*x* is P' can indeed be deduced from '*x* is', and in that sense is subsidiary to it. It is a defect of Christian's account that it gives no hint of this, and I suggest modifying his proposals so that the *existence* (reality, subsistence) of *x* (*y, z*) stands out as the crux. Clearly, conclusions accepted earlier in this study will influence the manner of the modification.

Now the burden of a fundamentally important argument of the study has been that, broadly speaking, the requirement of being justified in introducing transcendent entities (or, I would add, states) into a world-view is that there be some natural fact(s) calling for non-natural explanation. What this involves is a restriction upon and specification of the *kind* of support which facts must crucially give to basic religious proposals; and this must appear in the revised scheme of criteria.

In this respect (and others) the revised scheme will differ from Christian's by operating at a lower level of generality in the sense, not necessarily of being restricted to certain kinds of basic religious truth-claims, namely theistic ones, but of illustrating a more specific and detailed thesis regarding the conditions of truth of basic religious proposals. This represents in fact both a strength and a weakness of the revised scheme. It represents a strength in that it moves down from the level of useful but blunted generalities like 'the available facts give reasonably adequate support . . .', to a position where more contentious but sharper theses are presented of the type which ultimately is crucial in reaching a decision about basic religious truth-claims. It represents a weakness precisely in that· it is more contentious. On the other hand the scheme to be proposed is backed at all points by argument appearing somewhere or other in these pages, and it will be shown that the scheme represents a position of armed neutrality between religion and non-religion in general, and theism and non-theism in particular, which may be shared by both believers and non-believers. Thus the strength far outweighs the weakness.

What further criteria need to be mentioned at this point? The criterion of comprehensiveness is generally regarded as important and, interpreted for example as referring to the power of a basic proposal to do justice to the elements of truth in its logical alternatives, it should clearly be included.

Again it may be recalled that it is a necessary condition of religious truth that it mediate succour of some sort or, in traditional terminology, that it proffer salvation. Now this holds not only of developed doctrinal proposals or a whole doctrinal scheme, but also of basic religious proposals. Yet the notion of salvation must be fairly general, extending perhaps to cover notions of salvation in non-theistic religions too.

Three criteria of religious truth have been suggested by F. Ferré which jointly seem to supply just such a general sense.[5] Firstly, 'valuational adequacy' or 'richness' – acceptance of the proposal must not lead to the ignoring or distorting of values subscribed to with continuing, reasoned conviction as genuine, but should if anything reinforce them and indeed elicit new valuational responses of abiding and perhaps decisive significance (in the case of Christianity perhaps, for example, acceptance of being accepted in the divine love despite one's unacceptability). Secondly, 'valuational coherence' – the ability of the proposal to organise values and give them a coherent, integrated form capable of acting as the basis for coherent, integrated behaviour. Thirdly, 'valuational effectiveness' – the capacity to serve genuine life-needs rooted in basic human nature over long periods of time. Valuational adequacy is concerned with making life full; valuational coherence with making life whole; valuational effectiveness with the sustained success of both. In sum, religion should make life meaningful, and the meaning to be found in it is the general salvation it has to offer; though of focal significance will be a particular kind of salvation embedded in the general organism of belief corresponding to a particular analysis of basic human need – in Buddhism salvation from desire, in Christianity salvation from a paralysis of guilt perhaps, and from estrangement from God. In any event, these further criteria need to be included in the final scheme. Moreover they clearly relate to ongoing forms of religious life and experience, and this too should be mentioned. Clearly some mention will also be needed of principles of judgement concerned with value-assessment and value-ranking.

Yet if relevance to human needs is a necessary condition of religious truth, it would appear that some degree of such relevance is an equally necessary condition of a religious proposal's making a genuine truth-claim. That this is so then needs to be mentioned in A.

Finally, let me clarify the notion of a basic proposal. The following possibilities are relevant here:

Basic ramified religious proposal – X is P (e.g. the Christian God is holy).

Basic unramified religious proposal – x is P (e.g. God, whether Jewish, Moslem, Christian or whatever, is holy).

Basic ramified religious existential proposal – X exists (the Christian God exists).

Basic unramified religious existential proposal – x exists (God exists).

Basic metaphysical existential proposal – 'x' exists (a CEB exists).

Now in section B2 below I refer to 'the relevant basic existential proposal', and in section A I refer to a basic ramified or unramified existential proposal; and it might be thought that one of the latter two was being referred to in B2. Thus if the proposal under discussion in A were ramified, the proposal relevant in B2 would also be ramified; and if the proposal under discussion were unramified, so too would be the relevant proposal in B2. Yet not so – and if it were so, 'relevant' could simply be omitted. If the proposal whose truth one is seeking to warrant is ramified, the proposal relevant in B2 might be either ramified, or unramified, or metaphysical, as the example of the soft argument from contingency shows. If the proposal whose truth one is seeking to warrant is unramified, the proposal relevant in B2 might be either unramified or metaphysical.

Now clearly, if the relevant proposals in B2 are not identical with the proposals in A whose truth is being debated, the gap between them needs to be filled as the gap between the CEB and the God of Christianity was filled; and that it needs to be filled where it exists needs to be specified as one of the conditions connected with B2.

Drawing the preceding suggestions together, and drawing on the background provided by the whole of the present study up to this point, I suggest the following revised scheme of conditions of truth. It is clearly tailored to the theistic case which is my primary concern here. If perhaps, with minor adjustments, it should prove valid for other cases such as Brahman or Nirvana, as it may do, so much the better. Even if not, however, its validity for the theistic case remains unaffected. I realise that the scheme may appear to be unnecessarily long-winded or even forbidding, but I beg the reader's indulgence at this point, for behind its formality the scheme is in fact, I suggest, a convenient, accurate and indeed concise summary of the large number of methodological proposals developed and put into practice in this study.

A. It needs to be shown that some basic ramified or unramified religious existential proposal satisfies the conditions of making a significant religious truth-claim, namely:

- (i)   that it permits of self-consistent formulation;
- (ii)   that it permits the formulation of a self-consistent negation so that disagreement is possible;
- (iii)   that it permits some reference to its logical subject;
- (iv)   that some support for the existence of the logical subject is possible;
- (v)   that it exhibits some relevance to human needs.

B. It needs to be shown that in the circumstances we have sufficient warrant for accepting the proposal (i.e. since it is a proposal for belief, for making an affirmative judgement). This involves showing:

B1. That in the circumstances (including the general conditions of human life and the consequences of deciding or failing to decide between the proposal and its alternatives) the need for decision is sufficiently urgent; and

B2. That our warrant for the truth of the relevant basic existential proposal is sufficiently good, which means that:

(B2a) It is possible to make a reasonably successful and adequate reference to its logical subject; and

(B2b) The available principles of judgement are reasonably clear and complete; and

(B2c) The available facts give reasonably adequate support for affirming the existence of the logical subject, that is to say:

The existence of the logical subject is, or is capable of being treated as, a warranted explanatory hypothesis, that is to say:

(i) There are puzzling facts not totally explicable naturally and thus calling for non-natural explanation.

(ii) The existence of the logical subject explains these facts.

(iii) The existence of the logical subject explains these facts non-naturally.

(iv) The existence of the logical subject is (or, possibly, leads to) an explanatory ultimate.

(v) No available rival explanatory ultimate provides a better explanation.

(vi) Among possible equally explanatory available explanatory ultimates the concept of this logical subject is either the simplest or no more complex than can be warranted by good empirical fit (cf. B3 below).

(vii) The adoption of this relevant existential proposal as a suggestion for an explanatory hypothesis can if possible be supported by independent reasons rather than being dependent simply on the fact that the proposal is relevant to the proposal under debate in A.

(viii) Where appropriate, i.e. where the concept expressed by the subject is such that the existence of the logical subject is relevant to features of the world other than its mere existence or contingency, or to Qualitative features other than those which may appear in (B2c)(i), the existence of the logical subject is confirmed by loose empirical fit, which means that:

  (a)   the relevant principles of judgement are reasonably clear and complete;

  (bi)   there are transcendence-suggesting mysteries;

  ($b$ii)   the existence of the logical subject illuminates these mysteries;

  ($b$iii)   the mysteries are illuminated by the existence of the logical subject *qua* transcendent, that is, non-naturally;

  ($b$iv)   the existence of the logical subject is not obviously incompatible with any known natural fact or facts.

(ix) Where appropriate (*sic*), the existence of the logical subject is further confirmed by tight empirical fit subsequent to provisional acceptance of the proposal on the strength of the fulfilment of conditions (i)–(viii), which means that:

  (a)   the relevant principles of judgement are reasonably clear and complete;

  (bi)   there are mysteries, the interpretation of which as puzzles is licensed by provisional acceptance of the explanatory hypothesis, and which call for non-natural explanation;

  ($b$ii)   the existence of the logical subject explains these mysteries;

  ($b$iii)   The existence of the logical subject explains

these mysteries non-naturally;

(*b*iv) there are no, or no serious, transcendence-suggesting mysteries which the existence of the logical subject fails to illuminate;

(*b*v) the existence of the logical subject is not incompatible with any known natural fact or facts.

(B2*d*) The adoption of the relevant basic existential proposal as an explanatory hypothesis does not lead to incoherence.

B3. That where the relevant existential proposal in B2 is not equivalent to the proposal in A whose truth is the primary object of debate, there is sufficiently good warrant for identifying the logical subject of the former with the logical subject of the latter, which means that:

(B3*a*) The available principles of judgement are reasonably clear and complete; and

(B3*b*) The available facts give reasonably adequate support for the relevant development of the concept expressed by the subject term in B2, that is to say:

Development of tight empirical fit for the logical subject in B2 enables it to be identified with the logical subject in A, that is to say:

(i) There are mysteries the interpretation of which as puzzles is licensed by the warranted acceptance of the proposal in B2 and which call for, or suggest a need for, non-natural explanation.

(ii) The existence of the logical subject in B2 does not adequately explain these mysteries.

(iii) The existence of the logical subject of the proposal in A explains them.

(iv) The existence of the logical subject of the proposal in A explains them non-naturally.

(v) The existence of the logical subject in A is not incompatible with any known natural facts; and/or

(B3*c*) There are sound theoretical considerations which give reasonably adequate support for the relevant development of the concept expressed by the subject term in B2.

(B3*d*) The adoption of the proposal in A does not lead to incoherences.

B4. That where conditions (B2*c*)(viii) and (ix) are not appropriate to the relevant proposal in B2, they be applied to the proposal in A.

B5. That the basic proposal in A should mediate salvation, which means that:

(B5*a*) The available principles of judgement are reasonably clear and complete; and

(B5*b*) The proposal exhibits, or exhibits dispositions to,

(i) valuational adequacy;

(ii) valuational coherence;

(iii) valuational effectiveness; and

(B5*c*) The proposal connects with some form of the ritual dimension of religion.

Thirteen comments may be added by way of clarification:

1. Conditions (B2*c*)(i)–(ix) specify the nature of the support given by the facts. It may be felt that it is largely a question not of facts supporting a proposal but of setting it in orbit where it supports itself (*qua* explanatory). There is some truth in this, yet the actual setting in orbit, which is essential, is done by starting from facts calling for non-natural explanation, and remaining in orbit depends on the facts being explained. There is therefore no ground for legitimate dissatisfaction here.

2. If this study is correct, the explanatory hypothesis in (B2*c*) can be initially warranted only by the puzzling fact of ontological continuance, i.e. Existential considerations. Yet the scheme of conditions above is intended to allow the possibility of its being warranted by some major Qualitative consideration(s), with other and subsidiary Qualitative considerations in support forming empirical fit.

3. The condition is that principles of judgement be 'reasonably' complete because, as Christian observes, 'it is too much to ask that, in religious inquiry, any set of principles of judgement should be *complete* . . . this would be the case only for questions for which there is a calculus. In other cases "good judgement" is needed, whether in religion or in morality or in science.'[6]

4. The criterion of comprehensiveness referred to earlier is covered by the notion of empirical fit and also by conditions (B2*c*)(v) and (vi). Thus, although not mentioned explicitly, it is included and indeed expanded.

5. It is important to note that in B2 the existence of the logical subject either is *or is capable of being treated as* an explanatory hypothesis. Thus no violence is done to the non-hypothetical character of most religious beliefs as actually held by believers.

6. It might be argued that condition (B2c)(vii) should be deleted on the ground that what matters is not the origin of a hypothesis but its explanatory power; for no matter what the origin, the latter is not affected. Yet even if this be granted, independent reasons in support of entertaining a hypothesis cannot but enhance its respectability.

7. To the extent that the conditions in B3 are not fulfilled, to that extent the concept expressed by the subject term in A needs revision. On the other hand, to the extent that the conditions are fulfilled, to that extent perhaps the concept expressed by the subject term in A becomes more clearly defined; for the concept expressed by the subject term of a basic existential proposal is necessarily to some degree open-ended.

8. The notion of explanatory ultimacy is not included in that of empirical fit partly because it is catered for in earlier and more basic conditions, partly because there is no apparent end to qualitative questions as there is to world-contingency questions. 'Why is there a world?' leads to either a silly and sterile or to a recognisably ultimate 'Why is there a God?', but 'Why is the world ordered?' or 'Why is the world beautiful?' lead, it will be remembered, to parallel qualitative questions about God, like 'Why is God creative?', which are neither silly nor recognisably ultimate in their own right, but only by virtue of these features of the more basic question 'Why is there a God?' Alternatively expressed, the asking of 'existential' questions like world-contingency questions leads to a warranted existential ultimate; the asking of qualitative questions does not lead to a warranted qualitative ultimate independently of the former line of inquiry.

9. The 'mysteries' referred to in connection with empirical fit are intended to include major forms of religious experience.

10. Since condition B4 will operate only where the proposal in B2 is a basic metaphysical existential proposal (basic ramified and unramified existential proposals are both relevant to features of the world other than contingency), and since the proposal in A must be religious, condition B4 will always be

accompanied by condition B3, and in effect virtually amounts to urging that the arguments advanced in fulfilment of B3 be accorded confirmatory as well as concept-developmental status.

11. Inclusion of condition B5 makes explicit the need for natural theology in its total deployment to be richer and more closely related to the experiential, ritual, social and ethical dimensions of religion than much traditional natural theology. This connects with the eighth comment and the earlier discussion of religious experience.

12. Conditions (B2a), (B2c) and (B5b) differ from conditions A(iii)–(v) mainly in degree only.

13. The final comment is of fundamental importance and must be made at greater length. This account of conditions of truth presupposes or derives from acceptance of five principles of judgement which should not be confused with those within the scheme itself. They are, let us say, 'general' or 'external' principles of judgement, which differ from those 'internal' to the scheme in that they are presupposed by the scheme as a whole, and are not restricted to use in assessing the relevant facts and values within the scheme. The five principles are:

   I.   The principle of parsimony or Occam's razor.
   II.   The principle of natural explanation.
   III. The Stratonician principle.
   IV.   The Explanatory Principle.
   V.   The principle that the Explanatory Principle takes natural precedence over the other three.

All five principles have been backed by argument. Both their acceptance and their application may be eminently reasonable. Beyond that, however, still wider claims may be advanced on their behalf. There is no reason why they should not be taken to define an area of common ground between theists and non-theists, the features of which are further defined by the scheme of conditions of truth. Certainly that is the spirit in which the scheme is proposed. It is intended as a neutral account of conditions of theistic truth to which opponents may assent, a reasoned agreed context within which significant disagreement may occur and within which the true bones of contention may more easily be located.

This neutrality is, however, armed. The scheme will not please everybody and is ready to repel aggressors. The principle of natural explanation, for example, may come under attack from a variety of worthies concerned to preserve God's freedom of action from the arrogant encroachment of secularism. The Explanatory Principle may come under attack from over-sceptical non-theists who see it as the thin end of the theistic wedge. The account may be attacked in a variety of ways and is of course subject to correction by further argument. It may indeed be overthrown. But its defences are prepared and the contention here is that it is capable of withstanding destruction.

If this be basically sound, it follows that the rock-bottom fundamental causes of disagreement between theists and non-theists occur at points within the scheme. The further suggestion here is that they should be located in the internal principles of judgement.

It may be remembered that, as used by Christian, 'principles of judgement' cover rules of relevance, norms of judgement and a procedure for judgement. The last of these is barely mentioned by him and in this I follow suit. It is simply a matter of taking issues in turn (and deciding when their turn is). More valuable topics of analysis are rules of relevance and, in particular, norms of judgement. Let us consider them in the context of (B2*b*) in connection with the soft argument from contingency.

Two rules of relevance may be suggested:

(R1)   Consider those facts which seem to be, or which are or have been held to be, in need of non-natural explanation.

(R2)   Consider especially facts about the world as a whole which seem to be, or which are or have been held to be, in need of non-natural explanation.

These rules are of course neither proposed nor adopted arbitrarily but are backed by argument. Both rest on acceptance of the five external principles of judgement, the second particularly on the principle of natural explanation. There is little room for disagreement here provided these principles and the scheme itself have been accepted.

Five norms of judgement may be suggested:

(N1)   Intersubjective agreement about experiences, including contingency experiences, is a sign of their trust-
worthiness.

(N2)   In deciding whether a fact genuinely does call for
non-natural explanation, the natural precedence of
the explanatory principle over Occam's razor, the
Stratonician principle and the principle of natural explanation may, other things being equal, be used to
settle the issue; intellectual puzzlement apparently
insoluble by means of the Stratonician principle or
the principle of natural explanation indicates a need
for non-natural explanation.

(N3)   If there is evidence that a fact does need non-natural
explanation (for example, intersubjective agreement
about ontological shock, intellectual puzzlement apparently insoluble by means of the Stratonician principle or the principle of natural explanation), the fact
that it conceivably might not require non-natural explanation does not necessarily make it unreasonable
to suppose that it does, and . . .

(N4)   . . . in particular, it does not make it unreasonable to
suppose that it does if the puzzlement can be cured by
a non-natural hypothesis which is explanatorily rich
and plausible.

(N5)   Unless there be strong grounds to the contrary, in
non-natural explanation the ontological principle
should be adopted, namely the principle that, as
against abstractions, shadowy quasi-existents and
non-existents, 'actual entities are the only *reasons*'.[7]

These norms are also backed by argument (apart from the
fifth, which is not in fact crucial to the argument as developed
in Chapter 4), but unlike the rules of relevance they are subject to disagreement within the context of agreement about the
scheme as a whole. The view here is that, granted the factual
intelligibility of theism, they represent the deepest and most
proper nubs of disagreement between theists and non-theists.
The two sets of opponents cannot agree on (all) these norms
and still rationally maintain their opposed conclusions about
the truth or falsity of theism, as they can with the external

principles of judgement. Disagreement here is truly basic.

Since reasons may be presented both for and against norms of judgement, both their acceptance and rejection may be reasonable. Yet the reasons are unlikely to become anything approaching coercive. There will come a point here as elsewhere where further argument is futile, and there must be agreement to disagree, each side respecting the other. Perhaps interminable disagreement at this juncture, however, should be a lesser cause of dissatisfaction to the theist than interminable disagreement at any earlier stage. For at any earlier stage it should seem, if the present account is anywhere near correct, that the gulf between him and the non-theist is being constituted by less than essentials, that there is further ground for them to share; whereas here all the common ground possible has been charted, and it is in principle impossible for them to proceed together (except in so far as they may agree about some norms but not all, or not enough to justify one of them changing his belief). Then just as one parts more easily from a companion who has accompanied one as far as can reasonably be expected of him than from a companion who turns back or turns off sooner than hoped for, for reasons which seem less than satisfactory, so too the theist should here be more content to differ from his opponent than at any earlier stage. At worst the evangelical glint in his eye should here finally be extinguished.

Similar remarks could be made with regard to the other norms of judgement which appear in the scheme. In particular there is clearly scope for disagreement about the degree of tightness of empirical fit of a given proposal. In $(B2c)(ix)(a)$ for example, again in connection with the soft argument from contingency, two norms of judgement may be suggested. The first is non-controversial, given acceptance of the scheme as a whole; but the second is highly contentious:

($n1$)   Development of empirical fit must not exclude the principle of natural explanation; or
The precedence of the analogy between the world and a product of design over the analogy between the world and an atom or natural organism must not operate to the exclusion of the principle of natural explanation.

The significance of this is that, for example, the emergence of life as a transcendence-suggesting mystery cannot legitimately lead to the question 'Why did life emerge?' – that is a question permitting a complete answer in scientific terms – but must lead to a non-scientific question like 'Why is the world such as to produce life?'

(*n2*) Human will to live is an implicit affirmation of a pro-attitude to the world and to life which defuses the problems of pain and evil.

This is clearly quite unacceptable to many and perhaps rightly so.

In any event it is suggested here that most profitable debate should concern internal norms of judgement rather than external principles of judgement; not because the latter are less than crucial but because they are (or should be) less obstinate obstacles to a reasonable consensus.

So much by way of clarification of the scheme as it stands. It should not be thought, however, that this way of schematising the issue is the only correct one. The contention here nevertheless is that any different scheme should differ in form only and not in substance. Whether the substance might be better expressed by a rather different scheme remains an open question.

Yet one other way of expressing (B2*c*) is worthy of note in that it spotlights the logical form of the nerve of the kind of argument for the existence of God which is defended here in principle, and also in part at least in practice. That is to formulate (B2*c*) as follows: 'That the proposal is warranted by a sound transcendent-metaphysical abductive inference.' This may be explained conveniently in a separate section.

(ii) *The Form of the Argument*

'Abductive inference' is the label given by C. S. Peirce to a distinctive form of reasoning which he characterises thus:

The surprising fact C is observed,
But if A were true, C would be a matter of course;
Hence, there is reason to suspect that A is true.[8]

Peirce was concerned to show that reasoning towards a hypothesis differs from reasoning from a hypothesis but that the former, the proposing of a hypothesis, is in fact an inferential process and not simply a matter of chance or intuition. In point of fact, despite this straightforward account of Peirce's intention there are problems in pinning down just what 'abductive inference' is intended to cover.[9] For present purposes, however, this account will suffice.

The formulation quoted above describes a process which is inferential because the hypothesis 'is adopted for some reason, good or bad, and that reason, in being regarded as such, is regarded as lending the hypothesis some plausibility'. Now clearly the prime reason for its adoption is precisely that it apparently explains the surprising fact in question – though Peirce elsewhere asserts that it is 'also because the contrary hypothesis would probably lead to results contrary to those observed', and this leads to the point that abduction is not considered by Peirce to be a process which validates hypotheses. It goes no further than to provide grounds for a suspicion that a hypothesis may be true. Validation occurs by experimental testing, being the province of empirical verification/falsification. Thus a hypothesis should be 'such that definite consequences can be plentifully deduced from it of a kind which can be checked by observation'. This emphasis on experimental testing is entirely proper since Peirce is basically concerned with scientific reasoning.[10]

Now if the explanatory power of a hypothesis is a good reason for a suspicion as to its truth, this presupposes at the very least the principle of natural explanation, if not the Explanatory Principle itself. There is reason to suppose that Peirce would in fact have advocated the latter, as is done in the present study. According to Fann:

Peirce has consistently held, since 1868, that logic requires us to postulate of any given phenomenon, that it is capable of rational explanation (5.265). It is never allowable to suppose the facts absolutely inexplicable. Nothing justifies our abduction except its affording an explanation of the facts. It is no explanation at all to pronounce a fact inexplicable (1.139, 1.170, 8.168). That blocks the way of inquiry. Thus,

Peirce urges us to inscribe upon every wall of the city of philosophy the slogan: 'Do not block the way of inquiry' (1.135).[11]

Yet if the Explanatory Principle is taken seriously, it warrants a stronger form of abductive inference:

The surprising fact C is observed,
But if A were true, C would be a matter of course;
Hence, there is prima facie reason to accept A as true.

This could be further modified in a scientific context, the last line reading:

Hence, there is reason to accept A as true subject to (*a*) considerations of economy (i.e. no simpler hypothesis is sufficient) and (*b*) experimental confirmation.

That is to say, owing to its basis in the Explanatory Principle, abduction is itself a reason (however weak or provisional apart from the criteria embodied in the last line of the extended formulation of the inference) for accepting a hypothesis as true, not merely for proposing it or for entertaining a suspicion as to the possibility of its truth. Again, by expanding the inference in this way, the other criteria for assessing whether or not a given hypothesis is scientifically acceptable are allotted their crucial but rightly subordinate places in relation to abductive inference in its total deployment; 'rightly subordinate' because abduction is the mainspring of scientific inquiry, albeit insufficient.[12]

This modified form of abductive inference is explicitly scientific. Yet, granted the Explanatory Principle and the possibility of transcendent metaphysics, it is possible to formulate an outline valid form of transcendent-metaphysical abductive inference:

The surprising and in principle scientifically/naturally inexplicable fact C is observed,
But if A (referring to a *transcendens*) were true, C would be a matter of course;
Hence, there is reason to accept A as true provided that:
(i) It is possible to make a reasonably successful and adequate reference to A.
(ii) The available principles of judgement are reasonably clear and complete.

(iii)   A refers to (or refers to something that leads to) an explanatory ultimate.

(iv)   No available rival explanatory ultimate provides a better explanation.

(v)   Among possible equally explanatory available explanatory ultimates, A refers either to the simplest, or to no more complex a one than can be warranted by good empirical fit.

(vi)   As a suggestion for an explanatory role in an abductive inference A can if possible be supported by independent reasons, rather than being dependent simply on the fact that it is in someone's interest to suggest it.

(vii)   Where appropriate, A is confirmed by loose empirical fit.

(viii) Where appropriate, A is confirmed by tight empirical fit.

(ix)   Acceptance of A as an explanatory ultimate does not lead to incoherences.

Three comments only need to be added. Firstly, it should not be thought that condition (iv) changes the inference inappropriately – similar comparative elements are referred to by Peirce (cf. 2.628, quoted above). Secondly, condition (vi) is concerned with reasoning *to* a hypothesis, the others with reasoning *from* a hypothesis. It is therefore far from clear that it could be included in a punctilious imitation of Peirce's use of abduction. Since the latter is being used primarily as a springboard for a modified form of abduction, however, the condition may conveniently and properly be included in the transcendent metaphysical form of the inference. Thirdly, the second line of the inference, 'But if A . . ., C would be a matter of course', is intended to mean that A renders C *intelligible*. It is necessary to note this in order to avoid an argument such as the one that a patient's death (C) would be a matter of course if one posited that it had been predicted by a skilled physician (A); for such a prediction does not in itself, apart from the diagnostic grounds of the prediction, constitute a satisfactory explanation of the patient's death. The death might indeed in a sense be a matter of course; but it would not have been rendered intelligible.[13]

If these nine conditions are fulfilled (or as many as may be appropiate in a given case), belief in A is rationally warranted by a sound transcendent-metaphysical abductive inference. This is the logical form of the nerve of the argument(s) of natural theology providing a sound rational justification of theism.

It should be clear that abduction is distinct from deductive reasoning and from both inductive and hypothetico-deductive reasoning. Yet it is equally clearly a form of reasoning. It differs from hypothetico-deduction in that the hypothesis is justified by being explanatory without entailing empirically verifiable /falsifiable consequences. Empirical data are however clearly highly relevant. Granted that there are no insuperable obstacles in connection with factual meaning, an argument for the existence of God essentially in the form of a sound transcendent-metaphysical abductive inference would constitute a reasonably strong and adequate rational justification of theism. If the present study has been on the right lines it would appear to be basically the only sound methodological option available.

That it *is* the only sound methodological option available is however a stronger conclusion than is warranted here. For this study has by no means been exhaustive, and it is impossible to disregard totally for example the optimism expressed by P. Geach for a deductive causal argument, or even the possibility of a sound ontological argument.[14] Nevertheless the hope may be expressed that if such arguments should be formulated they would supplement the present approach rather than supplant it.

In any event recognition of abductive inference as a worthwhile form of justification should have a liberating influence. For it is all too frequently assumed or implied, by theologians and philosophers alike, that unless natural theology is either deductive or inductive it is worthless. Thus Tillich, for example, begins his *Systematic Theology* by urging that there is ample evidence that theology 'as an empirical-inductive or a metaphysical-deductive "science", or as a combination of both' is doomed, and that there comes a point where 'individual experience, traditional valuation, and personal commitment must decide the issue'; and Nielsen emphasises that 'the burden of proof is certainly on the theologian or philosopher . . . to show that there is some sound argument, deductive or inductive, for the existence of God'.[15] Other examples could be cited.

Now this bias in favour of deduction and induction has been shown here to be quite unwarranted with regard to natural theology, but it should be noted that liberation from the assumption that between them they exhaust the possibilities of inference is beneficial in other fields too. For example, writing of the evidence we have for the existence of the Sahara Desert when we have not been there, Pontifex writes: 'Individual witnesses may deceive us or may be deceived themselves, but it may become impossible to conceive of any explanation which would account for a vast number of witnesses deceiving us or being deceived themselves when they repeat the same story, except the explanation that the story is true.'[16] In effect, this is the outline of an abductive inference, employed epistemologically as a justification of (some of our) knowledge of the external world.

In such an inference lies too, I suggest, the solution both to the problem of our knowledge of the past, as is apparent from the earlier discussion of Russell's 'ten minutes ago' hypothesis, and also to the problem of other minds. If (crudely) I believe that I have a mind, then I am justified in believing that everyone else has one because this supposition explains more satisfactorily than any alternative supposition why all other people's bodies behave like mine – behaviour which is baffling if I suppose that they lack precisely what so often makes my body behave in the way that it does – and does not raise further problems such as why I should be the one exception in the animal kingdom.

Since the completion of this account (with the exception of the third comment above on transcendent-metaphysical abductive inference) there has appeared P. Achinstein's *Law and Explanation* which contains an excellent analysis of different forms of inference, including what he calls 'explanatory inference'. This is developed from Peirce's (and Hanson's) account of abductive inference (which he criticises), and is essentially like the account presented here except that it is oriented towards the role of abduction in science rather than in metaphysics. In addition to explanatory, deductive and inductive inferences, Achinstein furnishes an account of analogical inference and

analogical-explanatory inference. Thus the point made above
that deduction and induction do not between them exhaust the
modes of inference receives welcome and most impressive support.

Still more interesting perhaps is the large-scale support
given, in effect, by A. J. Ayer's Gifford Lectures. For the 'scientific approach' on which he there relies in order to cope with the
sceptic's arguments against our knowledge of the past, against
our knowledge of the external world, and against our knowledge of the existence of other minds, is in fact an expression of,
and practical vindication of relying on, abductive inference;
and reliance on the Explanatory Principle permeates the whole
work, apparently even to the extent of allowing the possibility of
what I have called a transcendent-metaphysical abductive inference.[17]

(iii) *The Character of the Argument*

Does this amount to a new-style natural theology, albeit differing drastically from the new style advocated by Macquarrie? In
part, but not altogether. It differs from much traditional natural theology in its insistence on relating the central metaphysical argument to major forms of religious experience, and the
conclusions reached to significant existential concerns and religious practice. In practice it differs too from much natural
theology by relating the various strands of argument together in
an organic whole – abductive inference inclusive of empirical fit
– rather than proposing independent arguments like, according
to a common interpretation at least, Aquinas's Five Ways; and
although of course this is dictated by what the evidence is taken
to permit, it has the merit that no problem arises as to whether
the entities reached at the end of different arguments may be
said to be one and the same – except perhaps in connection with
loose empirical fit. It differs again from much traditional work
by developing an explicitly soft argument which is intended to
be weaker in form, though stronger in substance, than the *a
priori* approach of ontological arguments and the near *a priori*
approach of some deductive cosmological arguments ('near *a
priori*' because they start not with a concept but with the fact
that something exists).

Closely related to ontological arguments of the Anselm,

Hartshorne and Malcolm type are those proposed by J. F. Ross, for example in his *Introduction to the Philosophy of Religion*, where God's necessity is deduced from his possibility. The deduction is no more successful, however, than in other attempts. We are asked to agree, for example, that 'it is possible that there is an accounting for the being of everything which exists that is capable both of being and of not-being'.[18] From this premise, and a second premise to the effect that any accounting for the being of things which are capable both of being and of not-being must be found ultimately in something which is not capable both of being and of not-being, i.e. a necessary being, the possibility of such a necessary being is deduced. But since 'no necessary being can be both possible and not actually existing (for then it would be contingent)', a necessary being must be actual or exist.

This last assertion is fatally ambiguous. Certainly a factually necessary being cannot be both factually necessary and not actually existing; but it may be the case both that a factually necessary being is possible, in the sense that 'factually necessary being' is a coherent concept and hence there is no (tenseless) logical impossibility in its having application, and yet also for it not to have application and for there to be no actually existing necessary being. Once this is appreciated, moreover, it is easy to uncover the same fallacy lurking in the seemingly innocent initial premise which in fact begs the basic question. For even if one accepts the second premise, then unless one already assumes that a necessary being exists, one cannot agree to the first interpreted in a way which yields the required conclusion – one cannot agree, that is, that 'it is [factually] possible that there is an accounting for . . .'. If the accounting for must be by means of a necessary being if it is to occur at all, and if the (factually) necessary being did not exist, such accounting for would be both a factual and a (tensed) logical *im*possibility (i.e. since it does not exist it is logically impossible that it should ever come to exist). The possibility of such impossibility will not be ruled out in advance by the open-minded inquirer once the issue is clearly pinpointed; consequently this 'formidable argument for the existence of the being which is God' falls rather flat.[19]

Nor can Ross win acceptance of the crucial premise by

introducing a principle of explicability to the effect that (crudely): It is logically possible that any given contingent state of affairs has an explanation. For this is equally and similarly question-begging. The only proper starting-point is; It *may be* logically possible that any given contingent state of affairs has an explanation. This begs no questions; but one cannot deduce from it that a necessary being exists.

Incidentally, no more than this is presupposed in the Explanatory Principle and its use in the soft argument from contingency. Moreover that argument has the advantage of being conducted in the light of a discussion of different types of explanation and their nature – a lacuna in Ross's book.[20]

Yet in thus developing a soft argument the present approach clearly has much in common with cosmic teleological approaches which on the whole have laid aside pretensions to coercive proof. Although explicitly non-coercive, however, it is not reducible to unconvincing exhortations to look about for 'pointers' to, or 'suggestions' of, divinity alone. On the contrary it has a reasonably strong inferential backbone, and in this is also a far cry from any form of Barthian revelationism or fideism, or Wittgensteinian acceptance of a form of life. This backbone is indeed essential. Remove it and the soft approach becomes mushy.

The present approach differs again from much traditional natural theology in that it does not move to a theistic conclusion from universally accepted (non-religious) premises such as Aquinas's 'Some things are in motion'. Rather, experiences of contingency and world-contingency questions are contentious. Now this is doubtless a comparative weakness of the present approach, and it is arguable that the approach is in fact an example of what Cobb calls a 'Christian' natural theology. According to Cobb a purely neutral starting-point for natural theology – such as 'Some things are in motion' – is today impossible, and consequently the natural theologian must take note of and accept the conditioned circularity of his position. For whether he realises it or not, his starting-point is conditioned by his Christian heritage and perspective on the world: compare Mascall's understanding and putative apprehension of the 'finiteness' of natural entities. Moreover the point about heritage is true even of non-Christian philosophers who develop or furnish the beginnings of a natural theology – Whitehead would appear to be an example of this.[21]

Yet while all this may be admitted, it does not follow that the conditioned circularity in question is necessarily vicious, for, as urged against Nielsen in Chapter 2, although the experience of contingency may primarily be due historically to a Christian outlook, it is not wedded to such an outlook, and may arise or be occasioned in those to whom such an outlook is foreign. Similarly, trust in the Explanatory Principle may have close historical ties with Christianity, but also be inherently trustworthy. If this were not so, and systematically not so with reference to other experiences and principles, some kind of Winch–Phillips position would after all be correct.[22] Yet since it is not correct it is at best misleading to label the present kind of approach a 'Christian' natural theology. For this label implies that the proponent of a natural theology for Christian theism necessarily stands somewhere inside the Christian circle of faith, and that in order for an outsider to be convinced by the proffered arguments he must first step inside the circle too – a view to which that defended here is expressly contrary. Let the influence of cultural heritage be acknowledged then; but let us speak rather of conditioned neutrality than of conditioned circularity, emphasising man's partial ability to transcend his limitations rather than his inability to transcend them entirely.

The present soft approach is not altogether dissimilar in principle from that advocated by J. Richmond in his programmatic *Theology and Metaphysics*. Richmond insists firmly and salutarily on the necessity of natural theology, a natural theology moreover which 'must be "explanatory": it must by necessity refer to the divine existence in order to explain what would otherwise be left puzzling attraction unclear: its intellectual attraction must reside in its power to make plain what is obscure.' There follows his 'tentative and comprehensive definition of natural theology: natural theology is the rational construction of a vision of the world as a whole, penetrating beyond the realm of appearances to that of ultimate reality, a divine order which is the sole explanation of an experienced world which would otherwise be left obscure, puzzling and unclear.'[23] This approach can thus certainly not be accused of lacking a backbone.

Nevertheless, upon closer examination it becomes apparent that the backbone is rather weak. Thus, for example, religious and moral experience are said to be areas calling for theological explanation, but it is not made clear why natural explanation is insufficient. Again, the quantity of intelligibility in the world is said to require non-natural explanation – a view which, as has been indicated, is insufficiently sensitive to the merits of Stratonician atheism.[24] Without entering further into the details of Richmond's case, it is perhaps not unfair to suggest that his programme fails to generate conviction in so far as basic questions concerning different types of explanation and their interrelations, and the relative strengths and weaknesses of fundamental principles like Occams's razor, the principle of natural explanation, and the Explanatory Principle, are left unasked.

The nub of disagreement may be further indicated by saying that Richmond's programme seems primarily, rather like Ramsey's and indeed Hick's, to amount in the end to a case for loose empirical fit only; for no indication is given of what could count as a puzzle genuinely calling for non-natural explanation, as opposed to a (mere) transcendence-suggesting mystery which by comparison is evidentially infirm. It is by no means incompatible with the soft approach advocated here, but even as a programme it needs crucial development. As it stands it is too soft to be serviceable.

Hick has suggested that in 'constructive apologetic the method changes, overtly or covertly, from impersonal demonstration to personal persuasion, from argument to recommendation', for there are no common scales in which to weigh the relative merits and demerits of theistic and anti-theistic evidences; 'it appears that the issue between them [the theist and the naturalist] is not one that can be settled by appeal to any agreed procedure'.[25] Yet this is over-sceptical of the merits of reason in assessing theistic truth-claims. It has been suggested here that theists and non-theists should be able to agree about the methodology outlined in the scheme of criteria, and to the extent that this occurs, to that extent the scheme and its external principles of judgement constitute common scales for use by both sets of protagonists. Moreover in striving for such agreement, arguments and counter-arguments are offered in support of and in opposition to the various principles of judgement, and while this is less than 'impersonal demonstration', it amounts to noticeably more than 'personal persuasion'. The alternatives are thus more varied than those offered by Hick.

The main element of truth in his contention may be expressed in the present context by saying that, to the extent that there is irreconcilable disagreement over internal norms of judgement, to that extent there are no common scales. Yet argument for and against the norms does not give way here either to mere 'recommendation'. It perseveres as argument – 'soft' and to that extent personal no doubt, which again reflects a measure of truth in Hick's view, but argument nevertheless. And when it is felt finally to fail, it gives way not to recommendation or persuasion, but to a truce. This is true too of course in connection with the external principles in so far as agreement on them is not achieved. There comes a point where, perhaps temporarily, perhaps permanently, the believer should admit that if the unbeliever cannot accept a particular principle or norm, he is right not to believe; and conversely. The purpose of the dialogue should be to see to what extent common scales can be constructed by joint reasoning and the exercise of judgement. To the extent that they cannot, the respectable alternative is to agree to differ, rather than to replace argument by recommendation and a kind of prescriptive seeing-as or experiencing-as which achieves nothing more substantial than to draw attention to loose empirical fit. Hick's proposal is sound in so far as it incorporates an implicit appeal for judgement, but it sadly underplays the role of reasoning and rational principles and the possibility of some kind of inferential argument. These defects render his approach, like Richmond's, too soft to be serviceable.

The criticisms levelled at Hick's account of the nature of the disagreement between theists and non-theists apply equally to Penelhum's account of the same, an account which is in fact basically a careful and instructive development of Hick's position.[26] Penelhum also contends, however, that the general consideration of parsimony does not enable one to prefer a naturalistic to a theistic interpretation of facts in the world, on the ground that while the naturalistic account does not multiply entities by introducing God, in some striking cases at least (presumably such as the Resurrection) its economy of entities must be weighed against its theoretical complexity (such a phenomenon is not easily explained but involves, for example, impressive 'coincidences and anomalies') and against 'the vague but recognisable claims of explanatory depth. The man who accepts that certain facts would prove God's existence or agency need not deny that naturalistic accounts of them can be given, but he will deny that they escape a fatal superficiality.'[27] By contrast, the view taken here is that to say that a natural explanation can be given of prima facie theistically evidential puzzles is to say that the natural explanation is complete and thus does not leave any facet of what is explained, nor any unexplained residue, for which a 'deeper' explanation is required. (The case of contingency is rather different, for this is not a facet or residue of a prima facie theistically evidential puzzle *qua* prima facie theistically evidential puzzle, but a facet of all natural occurrences *qua* natural.) With regard to the relative merits of parsimony of entities and theoretical complexity, preference for the former, in connection with transcendent beings at least, is enshrined in the principle of natural explanation, acceptance of which may be recommended, as by Miles, quite apart from the principle of parsimony.

The claim, then, is that if the present approach is soft it is far from mushy. The kind of justification offered, in principle and in part in practice, is non-coercive but firmly rational and inferential. Considerable and explicit scope for disagreement is balanced by continual emphasis on reasoned judgement.

Christian asks at one point what it would mean to be reasonable in religious arguments. His answer is as follows:

(*a*) It would mean being aware of the antecedent conditions of basic religious judgements, namely, the suppositions on which they are made and the questions they mean to decide. Put negatively, this means not making category mistakes of a certain sort, not confusing religious questions with scientific or moral or metaphysical questions. (*b*) It would mean also, if there are no *a priori* norms of judgement, not arguing as though there were some. Put positively, this means proposing our norms of judgement as subject to analysis and comparison with counterproposals. (*c*) It would mean also seriously looking for norms to which our opponents in argument might assent without being untrue to themselves, and trying to do justice to those facts which, rightly or wrongly, lead judgements.[28]

In all three ways the present approach can claim to be eminently reasonable. It indicates the kind of reasons appropriate for supporting theism, and the sort of way in which they count as reasons. It is intended (to use an unoriginal but useful metaphor) to provide a map of the disputed logical frontier between theism and atheism which may be acceptable to both camps in that it charts in greater detail than has hitherto been available stretches which may without loss of integrity be acknowledged by either side. It attempts to do full justice to the legitimate claims of modern atheism without capitulating to the kind of methodological imperialism practised by some empiricists. It attempts to give theism its due without retreating all the way from hard-headed rationalism to some brand of fideism, or even a weakly defended non-inferential religious reasonableness unacceptable in principle to non-believers. It seeks to overcome the kind of situation in which theists regard their opponents as short-sighted or insensitive, and atheists their opponents as at best obstinately muddled thinkers whose belief is based on faulty argument, the errors of which may be clearly exposed and equally clearly recognised by an incisive philosophical mind. If the views advanced in this study are anywhere near sound, the matter is not at all as simple as that. Theism and atheism owe each other considerably greater intellectual respect than is perhaps generally recognised – or even recognisable.

(iv) *Reason and Faith*

The relations between faith and reason constitute a traditional problem. It is hoped that the claims of reason in the vindication of theism have been firmly staked out. Despite earlier remarks it may be felt, however, that this soft natural theology cannot provide adequate grounds for faith.

If faith is defined in terms of absolute certainty, it must be admitted that it cannot. I would deny, however, that faith need be so defined; and there appears to be no reason why a soft natural theology judiciously presented should not generate and provide grounds for faith of rather more modest dimensions, yet of immense value to the believer, and also, it may be, to others; faith, that is, that is reasonably strong but not 100 per cent secure; faith involving perhaps a 'three-quarters belief' that God exists rather than a complete belief.[29] Nor will it do to object that this is nowhere near that saving belief which Christian belief should be; for in view of earlier remarks about the nature of salvation it may indeed be just that. Moreover it seems reasonable to suggest that if God exists he is aware of the epistemological difficulties of believing in him and cannot expect too much. It is an unexamined presupposition of many claims about both faith and salvation that he expects an all-or-nothing response, and should get it whatever the epistemological obstacles to be overcome. This is nonsense.

It should be clear that the most that could be warranted by an acceptable soft natural theology would be claims to belief rather than to knowledge. In order to substantiate the latter a closer approximation to conclusive evidence is required than a soft natural theology can furnish. Indeed, it is precisely absence of such evidence that has forced the move from hard to soft natural theology. Thus if a person who had come to believe on the basis, say, of the kind of soft natural theology proposed here, were to begin to make claims to have come to 'know' God in experience, the epistemological linchpin would remain the soft natural theology, not the knowledge-claims, even though this natural theology specifically suggests that God is experienced. Of course it is open to anyone to define *religious* 'knowledge' in a rather more lax manner than is customary in other fields and then claim such knowledge, but since nothing is gained by the move except a respectable misleading label, it seems futile.

10 The Existence of God

At the outset of this study I noted that there were to be three themes, one concerned with the methodology of justification, one concerned with the concept of God, one with assessing actual theistic truth-claims. Chapter 8 marked the close of the second theme, Chapter 9 virtually the close of the first. It remains to round off the third. Is the conclusion to be that belief in the existence of God is after all warranted, or the contrary, or that judgement should be suspended, or some other alternative? For a decision about this has hitherto carefully been avoided.

The soft argument from contingency to at least a creative CEB seems satisfactory. Yet if that were all, the matter might be left there as practically speaking irrelevant speculation; or its remoteness from everyday concerns might lead to its being ridiculed, and crucial norms of judgement which enable the conclusion to be reached (N3 and N4) might be replaced by strictly Stratonician norms. Yet that is not all. Empirical considerations enable the concept of the CEB to be filled out in a way that makes it relevant; and to some extent at least they act as confirmation of the existence of such a being, thereby indirectly supporting the relevant norms of judgement. The issue is therefore rather delicately balanced.

The question then arises whether condition B1 is fulfilled. Is the need for decision urgent? On an old-fashioned view of sin, salvation and judgement the answer is undoubtedly that a clear decision one way or the other is most urgent; but more charitable interpretations of the divine nature, not to mention human nature, suggest that it may not be. Nevertheless when one considers the importance of healthy religious belief in providing meaning and reinforcing moral endeavour, the need for decision increases. Moreover there is the point that if one opted for indefinite suspension of judgement, sooner or later one would probably find oneself living for all (or most) practical purposes as if there were no God, even if one felt insufficiently confident actually to advance the proposal that he did not exist. As it is sometimes put, one would be voting against God with one's life even if not with one's mind. One would not pray, for example, or only intermittently, and would not contribute to the worship and witness of Christian communities. There is thus a sense in which a decision one way or the other is unavoidable, the decision to suspend judgement proving by default to be a decision to act as if God were not. In this sense we are indeed faced, as W. James urges in 'The Will to Believe', with a forced option.

Yet this does not amount to a necessity for an outright intellectual acceptance or rejection of theism, only to a necessity to decide whether on the whole one is to conduct one's life either as if God does or as if God does not exist. In this highly important sense, therefore, we are not faced with a forced option – it is forced at the practical level only. Indefinite suspension of theoretical judgement is possible and may be justified. Thus if 'decision' in 'need for decision' is taken to mean a clear decision one way or the other, the need is not sufficiently urgent to justify such a decision come what may, or to justify going beyond the evidence to reach such a decision on other grounds, as advocated by James. (Though it might be. For example, if the genuine alternatives apparently lay between conducting one's life as though God existed and gaining heaven if he did, or simply ceasing if he did not; and conducting one's life as though God did not exist and being condemned to eternal hell if he did, or simply ceasing if he did not; then with this urgent necessity of clear decision, appeal to pragmatic grounds in making the decision in favour of theism would be in order. Certainly this would be to elevate self-interest over disinterested pursuit of truth, but in such a horrifying situation what price such disinterest? Given what to our eyes must seem a debased notion of God and of the religious meaning of life, Pascal's Wager rises to the situation superbly, impervious to the criticisms of its modern detractors which trade on a different religious understanding.) Yet the issue is sufficiently important to warrant trying to reach such a decision if at all possible. The question then arises as to just how delicately balanced an issue it is.

The argument of Chapters 4 and 5 supported the conclusion that the Christian God exists, only to stop short of the claim that the conclusion was actually warranted. This was necessary in view of the absence of specific analysis of the role of Qualitative arguments. Subsequent consideration of this topic served to confirm rather than undermine the conclusion, but despite this, in practice further attention needs to be devoted to particular theistically evidential areas of experience offered as confirmation, before the degree of confirmation can be deemed reasonably adequate. This is not to be undertaken in any detail here, but some of the important lines open to an apologist may very briefly be indicated or, where there has been occasion to mention them already, recalled. The considerations to which appeal is made are not novel, but if the present analysis of conditions of theistic truth is sound then they do not need to be; for basically the inadequacy of traditional natural theology lies not in the areas of experience chosen as theistically evidential, but in the elucidation of the way in which they count as evidence.

First, perhaps, it is quite staggering that the universe is such as to be capable of producing, and actually to produce, life in general and intelligent, personal life in particular. 'Being has so developed that it has been able through one of its minute manifestations, man, perhaps only at one tiny point in the universe and for but a moment, to turn back on itself, gather itself up from immense spaces and prodigious times, and think itself. If this is the result of an accident, rather than a convergence, it is an accident the contemplation of which leaves every man in awe.'[1] It is in order for the apologist to draw attention to this wonder and to the degree of order which it presupposes, and argue that it chimes in readily with the notion of an ultimate personal reality. There is a plausibility about this argument which allows it to qualify as an element in support of a claim to loose empirical fit. And if the existence of a personal creator is provisionally accepted, the development of intelligent life in the cosmos, treated now as a genuine puzzle, may be further illumined, thereby allowing the empirical fit to become tighter. For example, it is intellectually satisfying to solve the problem in terms of a personal creator creating persons, and indeed creating in their way personal creators, because he prizes such personality and creativity for their own sakes, and prizes our prizing them for their own sakes; and uneasiness about this explanation on account of the felt insignificance of man in the immensities of space and time may be conquered by emphasis on human ability to know the immensities, to manipulate his environment, and on the possible significance of those immensities as mediating symbols of the majesty of God. Moreover, proper tribute could be paid in such an account to non-human animal achievement.

This view leads, however, to further questions of value. There is the beauty of the cosmos, for example, which is perhaps almost universally acknowledged and which immediately confers a measure of credibility on the notion that it is the product of an intelligence which holds sublimeness dear – an element in support of loose empirical fit. Provisional acceptance of the existence of such an intelligence strengthens the evidence by licensing its interpretation as a puzzle rather than a mystery.

Any attempt by an apologist to capitalise on this particular puzzle should be heavily indebted to Tennant's outstanding treatment of the topic. Speaking of 'the saturation of Nature with beauty', he continues:

> On the telescopic and on the microscopic scale, from the starry heaven to the siliceous skeleton of the diatom, in her inward parts (if scientific imagination be veridical) as well as on the surface, in flowers that 'blush unseen' and gems that the 'unfathomed caves of ocean bear', Nature is sublime or beautiful, and the exceptions do but prove the rule.

If we take this beauty to be the fortuitous concomitant of blind cosmic forces we are struck by the contrast between the aesthetic achievement of these forces and human facility in generating ugliness unless specifically engaged in an attempt to the contrary:

> Here, then, are two kinds of agency, *ex hypothesi* proceeding with indifference to the realisation of aesthetic values: we might almost say the one never achieves, while the other never misses, the beautiful. And the same contrast subsists

between their processes as between their products. Compare, e.g., 'the rattling looms and the hammering noise of human workshops' with Nature's silent or musical constructiveness; or the devastating stinks of chemical works with Nature's fragrant distillations.

The hyperbole in this does not destroy its truth. 'In the very act of labouring as a machine [Nature] also sleeps as a picture.'[2] Drawing his conclusion Tennant continues: 'If "God made the country" whereas man made the town – and the black country – we have a possible explanation of these things; but if the theism contained in this saying be rejected, explanation does not seem to be forthcoming.'

Yet in addition the matter may be pursued on a slightly different tack: 'It may further be observed that, in so far as the mechanical stability and the analytic intelligibility of the inorganic world are concerned, beauty is a superfluity. Also that in the organic world aesthetic pleasingness of colour, etc., seems to possess survival-value on but a limited scale.'[3] The latter contention is strikingly illustrated in the following passage, written while its author was observing a gay procession of ducks and geese on Regent's Park lake. He considers the explanation

that the hues and patterns which those water-fowl display have been evolved by the slow and uncertain process of sexual selection. According to this theory it is the birds who are the artists and who possess such consummate taste. By discriminate choosing of their mates those Chinese geese, which are gliding past me now, have produced that superb pencilling on their wings, that pale edging to each feather and that delicate tinting of their necks which awake in me such intense aesthetic pleasure. So unerring and so insistent has been their judgement that it has been able to override the blind compulsions of sex and, after many generations, to produce a work of art. I find it impossible to believe that the miracle of their loveliness could have been wrought by the sexual discrimination of those geese, more especially when the scientists tell me that animals possess little or no sense of colour. But even if the geese possessed this sense, would their feeling for design be so strong as to overcome all other desires? It is not so with human artists and Darwin himself stated that: 'In all ordinary cases the male is so eager that he will accept any female, and does not, as far as we can judge, prefer one to the other; but . . . exceptions to this rule apparently occur in some few groups.'[4]

If this view be well-founded, there would indeed appear to be some justification for regarding the development of animate beauty as in significant measure an exception to the principle of natural explanation – the justification lying in its superfluity as part of a natural explanation of animal development. Yet quite apart from that, the beauty to which attention is drawn retains significance.

The force of these considerations is in no way weakened by the contention that beauty is 'subjective'; for whatever truth this contention may contain, it remains a fact that we cannot see beauty wherever our fancy pleases; and more basically the fact remains that nature is such as to evoke recurrent aesthetic reactions of wonder and awe from beings such as ourselves, though less satisfying alternatives are conceivable, and though products and processes of human industry begotten of other than aesthetic purposes more often than not fail to do so. All this is striking indeed.

Tennant further observes that 'if we do apply this category of design to the whole time-process, the beauty of nature may not only be assigned a cause but also a meaning, or a revelational function. . . . From its very origination religious experience seems to have been conditioned by the impressiveness or the awesomeness of natural phenomena, suggestive of an invisible and mysterious presence.'[5] Here we come to a third significant area of experience. The fact that intimations of a transcendent presence have been and are felt and reported neither renders the theistic hypothesis less plausible nor leaves it unaffected; on the contrary, it supplies a further important element in loose empirical fit. Provisional acceptance of the hypothesis strengthens the evidence, and the further discovery (if such it be) that the hypothesis is uniquely able to illuminate all major forms of religious experience, as argued in N. Smart's natural theology of religious experience, again significantly reinforces the degree of confirmation which this area of human experience is able to supply. For it is a sound methodological principle and norm of judgement that a world-view which, without violating other basic methodological principles, does not undermine vast tracts of valuable human experience, is greatly to be preferred to world-views which are thus subversive.

Over and above this the Christian apologist may claim that there are some religious experiences of a striking character which are illumined by the theistic hypothesis in such a way as to suggest focal revelation on the part of the deity – namely those experiences attributed to Jesus. This both adds to the confirmation provided by religious experience in general by virtue of its striking particularity, and is highly significant in confirming Christian claims about his character.

In each of these cases we are faced with a striking and prima facie puzzling fact which seems most hospitable to interpretation in theistic terms, and whose evidential strength is increased by being treated, subsequent to provisional acceptance of the theistic hypothesis, as a genuine puzzle which this hypothesis strongly illumines.

In addition we may mention an issue which bears on the overall coherence of the hypothesis, and this is the all-embracing issue of the meaning of life. As was emphasised earlier, life may be full of meaning quite apart from religion. It has to be admitted, however, that without religion life's meaningfulness stands against a backdrop of cosmic meaninglessness. 'We find the universe terrifying because of its vast meaningless distances, terrifying because of its inconceivably long vistas of time which dwarf human history to the twinkling of an eye, terrifying because of our extreme loneliness, and because of the material insignificance of our home in space – a millionth part of a grain of sand out of all the sea-sand in the world.'[6] The result is a conflict between what may be called the domestic and cosmic perspectives, and the need to choose one to the exclusion of the other.[7]

Now from a viewpoint within theistic religion there is no clash between these perspectives. The need for choice disappears as they are harmonised in one over-arching vision of the cosmos as a God-given home. Moreover this vision enriches the domestic perspective too, in eliciting worship for example; or in opening up possibilities of ultimate meaning for otherwise apparently irredeemably meaningless lives; or tingeing everyday values and concerns with a religious overplus of value – the artist, for example, may be seen as co-creator of beauty and value with God, and both creation and enjoyment of artistic beauty may be interpreted as oblique acts of worship, being respectively the development of the world's God-given potentialities for further beauty and the celebration of their realisation: thus in this sense the thrill and exultation experienced, for example, at the climax of Beethoven's Ninth Symphony may be interpreted and valued as religious exaltation.

This is of course significant not only with regard to coherence but also with regard to condition B5; for the ability of the theistic hypothesis to enhance and deepen life's meaningfulness is some measure of its ability to mediate salvation. Highly significant in this respect too is Christian theism's ability to supply practical moral reinforcement in the form of divine presence and succour, and both reinforcement and perhaps illumination in the inspiring example furnished by Jesus. Moreover it is not otiose to interpret morality in terms of submission to God's will, given that God is good and may be presumed to know what is right in a given situation by knowing all the relevant circumstances; and while this supplies neither a short-cut to moral decision nor a missing theoretical backing to moral precepts, it does impart to morality a certain personal warmth, not least by abrogating the otherwise insuperable loneliness of much moral decision and endeavour. Again, in a way which connects with the problem of the occurrence of intelligent life, moral goodness as an intrinsic value illumines the appearance of such life by providing axiological justification.

In these areas of experience at least, then, it seems possible to muster a significant degree of confirmation of the hypothesis that God exists, though clearly the argument needs development. It is worth mentioning that in such development two epistemological techniques elucidated by J. Wisdom may be valuable.[8] The 'connecting technique' consists of drawing attention to less than obvious relations between certain features, as may be illustrated by Richmond's example of 'the author who cross-indexes his manuscript with the purpose of drawing attention to connections between apparently diverse and unconnected passages, connections which in his view give the work a pattern, an overall meaning or impact which might easily be missed'. Something of this is apparent in Smart's interpretation of religious experience, for example. Richmond adds significantly: 'The *connections* thus established become heuristic. . . .' The 'disconnecting technique' consists of breaking down misconnections. In isolation from inferential justification these techniques are methodologically insufficient for grounding theistic belief by virtue of being inadequately sensitive to the virtues of Occam's razor – the by now familiar point that, all things being equal, a non-theistic seeing-as should be preferred to a theistic seeing-as. Yet in conjunction with inferential justification their merits are considerable.

Wisdom speaks too of features of a case which '*severally co-operate* in favour of the conclusion', of reasons which act 'like the legs of a chair, not the links of a chain', of reasoning that is 'not *vertically* extensive but *horizontally* extensive'.[9] In the soft approach advocated here, the abductive inference operates rather like a chain of reasoning (albeit non-deductive), the arguments in support of empirical fit like chair-legs and cumulative in effect. Or, to introduce another image, the rational justification of theistic belief is rather like a certain tropical or subtropical tree – the argument from contingency (in the present case) forms the main trunk, but the great superstructure of the tree, the theistic conclusion, is supported too by other minor trunks which surround the main trunk at some distance from it, and these are the arguments in support of empirical fit.

The Wisdomian view expressed by F. Waismann with regard to philosophical argument in general is also highly instructive in relation to the task of the apologist or inquirer, particularly in developing empirical fit and reaching a conclusion; so much so, indeed, that it is worth quoting at some length. Having opposed the view that philosophers in the main advance 'proofs and refutations in a strict sense', he urges that

> what the philosopher does is something else. *He builds up a case.* First, he makes you see all the weaknesses, disadvantages, shortcomings of a position; he brings to light inconsistencies in it or points out how unnatural some of the ideas underlying the whole theory are by pushing them to their farthest consequences; and this he does with the

strongest weapons in his arsenal, reduction to absurdity and infinite regress. On the other hand, he offers you a new way of looking at things not exposed to those objections. In other words, he submits to you, like a barrister, all the facts of his case, and you are in the position of the judge. You look at them carefully, go into the details, weigh the pros and cons and arrive at a verdict. But in arriving at a verdict you are not following a deductive highway, any more than a judge in the High Court does. Coming to a decision, though a rational process, is very unlike drawing conclusions from given premisses, just as it is very unlike doing sums. A judge has to judge, we say, implying that he has to use discernment in contrast to applying, machine-like, a set of mechanical rules. There are no computing machines for doing the judge's work nor could there be any – a trivial yet significant fact. When the judge reaches a decision this may be, and in fact often is, a rational result, yet not one obtained by deduction; it does not simply follow from such-and-such: what is required is insight, judgement.[10]

The present approach differs from this general view by specifying definite conditions of truth to be fulfilled, among which the role of abductive inference is given due prominence. Nevertheless the parallels are sufficiently close to be highly instructive, particularly in connection with empirical fit and reaching a conclusion.

As was made clear earlier, it is advocacy of an abductive inferential backbone as an essential supplement to a more loosely structured Wisdomian approach that differentiates the present position from the approaches of Hick and Penelhum. It is therefore encouraging to find that the most recent contribution to developing a Wisdomian approach does in effect include such a backbone. In his *The Justification of Religious Belief*, B. Mitchell emphasises (with Wisdom and Waismann, though really against Hick and Penelhum) the *rationality* of cumulative argument, and refers to the criteria of 'consistency, coherence, simplicity, elegance, *explanatory power*, fertility'.[11] Mitchell does not, however, develop this aspect of his case, and seems indeed in the end to be making proposals essentially similar to Richmond. Although I have started from the other end, so to speak, my own proposals and theirs may thus be regarded as being in effect mutually complementary. Mitchell's defence of the status of theistic belief as a *hypothesis*, in chap. 7 of his book, is of particular relevance and value in connection with the argument presented here.

Returning now to the areas of experience discussed in connection with empirical fit (there are doubtless others), taken together with the argument from contingency they furnish a reasonably impressive body of evidence not lightly to be dismissed. As a body they provide the theist with his answer to the legitimate, comparatively weak empiricist challenge: What would have to be different in order for 'God exists' to be intellectually untenable? Primarily there would have to be an absence of the relevant experiences of contingency, and perhaps further reason for supposing tensed world-contingency questions to be silly. Subsidiarily but significantly there would have to be absence of a high degree of order, absence of (paradoxically) life and intelligence, absence of beauty, absence of religious experience – in short, absence of a basis for an analogy between the world and a product of intelligent design. This would not disprove the existence of God but it would rob theistic belief of all intellectual warrant.

Yet as things are, is the warrant sufficient? Conditional upon the tractability of the problem of evil perhaps it is. Certainly, theistic belief should not be written off completely, as in some quarters, on the grounds that none of the proposed evidence and argument is any good at all. Yet in the absence of discussion of the problem of evil, perhaps the most appropriate conclusion is 'not proven' in a sense analogous to that in which the phrase is used in Scottish courts. It is adopted in cases where the evidence is insufficient to warrant a verdict of 'guilty', but sufficiently weighty to make a verdict of 'not guilty' seem wrong. In the present case the evidence summoned appears sufficiently impressive to make an outright verdict of 'not true' seem reckless, yet very proper misgivings about the problem of evil militate against an outright verdict of 'true'. Both aspects are fully accommodated by a verdict of 'not proven', with its implication that, of the other two alternatives, 'true' is nearer the mark than 'not true'.

Yet despite this implication, just as in the law-court 'not

proven' is practically speaking equivalent to 'not guilty' in that it ends in acquittal, so here in connection with Christian theism, except as a temporary measure, it is practically speaking equivalent to 'not true'. For if one adopted it as a permanent conclusion, one's life-style would tend strongly to be non-Christian; non-Christian in the sense that there would be no prayer life, no worship, no general experiencing-as in a Christian way, no attempt to be any kind of 'Christian witness' – or at any rate no attempt to sustain any of these. Of course one's life-style would differ too from that of convinced atheists for whom the verdict 'not true' is an article of faith: in that sense there are degrees of voting against God with one's life. Nevertheless, permanent acceptance of 'not proven' as a conclusion would be accompanied by to a greater or lesser degree tentative practical commitment to 'not true'; a commitment which, depending on the degree of tentativeness, would stand over against, and in some tension with, the conclusion and its positive implications. If at all possible, therefore, unless these implications are to be weakened, the conclusion should give way to its positive alternative; and in this respect it is salutary to recall Bishop Butler's famous advice:

> In questions of difficulty . . . where more satisfactory evidence cannot be had or is not seen, if the result of the examination be that there appears upon the whole even the lowest presumption on one side and none on the other, or a greater presumption on one side, though in the lowest degree greater, this determines the question, even in matters of speculation; and in matters of practice will lay us under an absolute and formal obligation, in point of prudence and of interest, to act upon that presumption or low probability – though it be so low as to leave the mind in very great doubt which is the truth.[12]

Should it be felt impossible to follow this advice, however, perhaps because one wishes after all to weaken the positive implications of the 'not proven' verdict, and if outright rejection of Christian theism continues to be avoided, this intermediate conclusion is a perfectly legitimate and respectable resting-place despite its element of tension, for this need never amount to inconsistency. Indeed, at the risk of a little repetition, it should be emphasised that an intermediate position rationally ought to be embraced permanently in the (doubtless relatively unlikely) event of a complete deadlock between evidence *pro* and *contra*, rather than being avoided by appealing to one's personal preferences as advocated by James. Certainly the introduction of such evidential deadlock would strengthen his case considerably. For although it seems to be implicit in it when he speaks of 'a genuine option that cannot by its nature be decided on intellectual grounds', it is not included in his definition of a 'genuine option' as 'living', 'forced' and 'momentous'; and this provides an opening and some justification for the criticism that his argument, taken to its logical conclusion, 'authorises us to believe . . . any proposition, not demonstrably false, which it might be advantageous to us, in this world or another, to have accepted'.[13] James's attempt to 'narrow our licence for gratuitous belief' by restriction to living options, that is, to propositions which we have a pre-existing tendency to believe, is said to be worthless, for the origins of this tendency may be pure accidents, for example of geographical location, belief in Muhammad being a living option to an Arab and not, let us say, to an Amazon Indian. This is true, but it would be possible to take 'living' as involving some reference to plausible grounds of belief, and the option that cannot be decided on purely intellectual grounds as a proposition for and against which the evidence seems equally plausible. Hick's (and other) criticisms would then be circumvented. Yet even then the kind of pragmatic procedure advocated by James for settling the issue, in favour of theism let us say, should not be adopted; for the result would be a belief in God which was logically unacceptable in that it lacked rational justification: one would be accepting the evidence *pro at the expense of* the evidence *contra*. In addition, of course, there might well be problems of psychological acceptability: having proceeded thus far with one's inquiry, the attempt to cap it by believing without sufficient evidence might well not work, not at any rate in the long run. Whether or not the procedure would be morally repugnant (compare Owen's condemnation of Pascal's Wager as 'logically, psychologically, and morally intolerable') would presumably depend on its motivation.[14]

In any event, the present general conclusion may be put as

follows. Given a measure of tractability in the problem of evil, outright rejection of Christian theism with a straight verdict of 'not true' does less than full justice to the evidence in its favour. A verdict of 'not proven' at least may be passed. It would not be unreasonable to plump for tentative commitment to Christian theism as a working hypothesis, with a to a greater or lesser degree faltering verdict of 'true'.

Postscript

I have been discussing the *rational* grounds of belief in God. Yet it is quite clear that actual decisions for or against such belief are not taken purely in the realm of pure intellectual reasoning. The inquirer is influenced by the atmosphere of the concrete historical community in which he conducts his quest, and by his place in that community.

Entertain now for a moment the indubitably false propositions that everything that I have written here is true, that everyone who ever reads the book is going to agree that it is true, and that after reading the book they are going to come to reasonably final conclusions about the truth or otherwise of Christian belief. They will nevertheless reach divergent conclusions because of their varying historical and personal situations. I do not think that we can avoid this being so; nor do I think that we should torment ourselves, or taunt each other, that it is so. It does not matter. A decision for atheism can be as valuable in one concrete historical situation as a decision for (some form of) Christianity in another; and I see no reason why God, if he exists, should not need atheists in some situations as much as Christians in others. After all, according to Christianity itself, at least as I understand it, we shall in the end be judged, not according to how much knowledge we have acquired in matters of specifically religious truth, but according to how much we have loved.

On the other hand I do not believe that a book such as this is therefore irrelevant, for I have in no way intimated either that cultural (or personal) conditioning amounts to cultural (or personal) determinism, or that the process of reaching a decision is insignificant.

Notes

Chapter 1

1. J. Macquarrie, *Principles of Christian Theology* (London: S.C.M. Press, 1966) pp. 45–50 ff.

2. R. W. Hepburn, 'The Gospel and the Claims of Logic', in *Religion and Humanism* (London:B.B.C., 1964) p. 16.

3. Cf. N. Smart, *Reasons and Faiths* (London: Routledge & Kegan Paul, 1958) pp. 44–5.

4. Cf. S. Lukes, 'Some Problems about Rationality', and M. Hollis, 'The Limits of Irrationality', in B. Wilson (ed.), *Rationality* (Oxford: Blackwell, 1970); J. Shepherd, 'The Contextualisation of Criteria', forthcoming in *Sophia*.

5. R. W. Hepburn, 'Mysticism, Nature and Assessment of', in P. Edwards (ed.), *The Encyclopaedia of Philosophy* (New York: Macmillan, 1967) v, p. 433. The Eckhart reference is to his *Sermons*, p. 202.

6. T. R. Miles, 'On Excluding the Supernatural', *Religious Studies*, I (April 1966) 146–7.

7. Ibid.

8. K. Popper, *The Logic of Scientific Discovery* (London: Hutchinson, 1959). Cf. P. B. Medawar, *The Art of the Soluble* (Harmondsworth: Penguin Books, 1969) pp. 127–73.

9. I. T. Ramsey, *Religion and Science: Conflict and Synthesis* (London: S.P.C.K., 1964) pp. 70–1.

10. J. Baillie, *The Interpretation of Religion* (Edinburgh: T. & T. Clark, 1929) p. 94; A. Farrer, *Finite and Infinite*, 2nd ed. (London: Dacre Press, 1959) p. 3.

11. J. Cook Wilson, 'Rational Grounds of Belief in God', reprinted in N. Smart (ed.), *Historical Selections in the Philosophy of Religion* (London: S.C.M. Press, 1962) p. 440.

12. Cf. R. W. Hepburn, *Christianity and Paradox* (London: Watts, 1958) pp. 206–7.

13. H. D. Lewis, *Our Experience of God* (London: Allen & Unwin, 1959) p. 102.

Chapter 2

1. The first four are mentioned by H. P. Owen in his *The Christian Knowledge of God* (London: Athlone Press, 1969) pp. 80–1.

2. L. Wittgenstein, *Tractatus Logico-philosophicus*, trans. D. Pears and B. F.

McGuiness (London: Routledge & Kegan Paul, 1922) 6.44; N. Malcolm, *Ludwig Wittgenstein: A Memoir* (London: Oxford Univ. Press, 1958) p. 70.

3. J. J. C. Smart, 'The Existence of God', in A. Flew and A. MacIntyre (eds.), *New Essays in Philosophical Theology* (London: S.C.M. Press, 1956) p. 46.

4. I. M. Crombie, 'The Possibility of Theological Statements', in B. Mitchell (ed.), *Faith and Logic* (London: Allen & Unwin, 1957) p. 65; K. Nielsen, 'On Fixing the Reference Range of "God" ', *Religious Studies*, II (Oct. 1966) 26–7.

5. Nielsen, ibid., p. 27.

6. M. K. Munitz, *The Mystery of Existence: An Essay in Philosophical Cosmology* (New York: Appleton-Century-Crofts, 1965) pp. 45–7.

7. Wittgenstein, *Tractatus*, 6.5.

8. Owen, *Christian Knowledge of God*, p. 84; C. B. Martin, *Religious Belief* (Ithaca N.Y.: Cornell Univ. Press, 1959) pp. 156–7.

9. Munitz, *Mystery of Existence*, p. 144; N. Smart, *Reasons and Faiths*, p. 51.

10. H. Bergson, *Creative Evolution*, trans. A. Mitchell (London: Macmillan, 1911) pp. 293 ff., esp. p. 299.

11. R. Carnap, 'The Elimination of Metaphysics through Logical Analysis of Language', in A. J. Ayer (ed.), *Logical Positivism* (Glencoe Ill.: Free Press, 1959) p. 71.

12. N. L. Wilson, 'Existence Assumptions and Contingent Meaningfulness', *Mind*, XV (1956) 343.

13. Munitz, *Mystery of Existence*, p. 156.

14. 'Consequential' as K. Baier calls it; see his *The Meaning of Life*, Inaugural Lecture (Canberra, 1957) pp. 7–8.

15. Munitz, *Mystery of Existence*, part 4.

Chapter 3

1. H. D. Lewis, *Teach Yourself Philosophy of Religion* (London: English Universities Press, 1965) p. 144.

2. Lewis, *Our Experience of God*, pp. 43, 41.

3. Lewis, *Philosophy of Religion*, p. 14.

4. E. L. Mascall, *He Who Is: A Study in Traditional Theism* (London: Darton, Longman & Todd, 1966) p. 85; *Existence and Analogy: A Sequel to 'He Who Is'* (London: Darton, Longman & Todd, 1966) p. 80.

5. Mascall, *He Who Is*, p. 80.

6. Mascall, *Existence and Analogy*, pp. 89, 90.

7. Mascall, *Words and Images: A Study in Theological Discourse* (London: Darton, Longman & Todd, 1968) pp. 84–5; cf. *The Openness of Being: Natural Theology Today*, Gifford Lectures (London: Darton, Longman & Todd, 1971) pp. 110–11, cf. pp. xi, 14.

8. M. Pontifex, *The Existence of God: A Thomist Essay* (London: Catholic Book Club, 1949) p. 31.

9. Owen, *Christian Knowledge of God*, p. 81.

10. Ibid., pp. 78–9.

11. Ibid., pp. 85–6.

12. Ibid., p. 78.

13. Ibid., p. 79.

14. Ibid., p. 253; T. Penelhum, 'Divine Necessity', *Mind*, LXIX (April 1960) 181.

15. Mascall, *Openness of Being*, p. 49.

Chapter 4

1. Jerome A. Shaffer, *Philosophy of Mind* (Englewood Cliffs, N.J.: Prentice-Hall, 1968) p. 93, cf. pp. 91–4, 97–106.

2. Martin, *Religious Belief*, pp. 152–6; J. Hospers, 'What Is Explanation?' in A. Flew (ed.), *Essays in Conceptual Analysis* (London: Macmillan, 1956) pp. 116–17.

3. A. Flew, *God and Philosophy* (London: Hutchinson, 1966) 5.8. The reference is to N. Smart, *Philosophers and Religious Truth* (London: S.C.M. Press, 1964).

4. F. R. Tennant, *Philosophical Theology* (Cambridge Univ. Press, 1930) II, p. 128; S. Alexander, *Space, Time and Deity*, Gifford Lectures (London: Macmillan, 1920) I, pp. 281–2.

5. P. Edwards, 'The Cosmological Argument', in *The Rationalist Annual, 1959* (London: Watts, 1958) p. 71.

6. Flew, *God and Philosophy*, 3.20.

7. This is contested by some, eg. Flew in his 'Divine Omnipotence and Human Freedom', in Flew and MacIntyre (eds.), *New Essays in Philosophical Theology*, pp. 144–69. Among numerous critiques of Flew's position may be mentioned F. Ferré, *Language, Logic and God* (London: Eyre & Spottiswoode, 1962) pp. 116–20, and N. Smart, *Philosophers and Religious Truth*, 3.11–20.

8. Smart, ibid., 4.27; Munitz, *Mystery of Existence*, p. 259; Flew, *God and Philosophy*, 5.8.

9. Smart, ibid., 4.27.

10. J. Hick, *Arguments for the Existence of God* (London: Macmillan, 1970) pp. 50, 49, cf. pp. 46–52; cf. G. F. Woods, *Theological Explanation* (Welwyn: Nisbet, 1958).

11. Tennant, *Philosophical Theology*, II, p. 212.

12. F. R. Tennant, *Miracle and its Philosophical Presuppositions* (Cambridge Univ. Press, 1925) p. 50. Cf. Tennant, *Philosophical Theology*, II, chap. 7 and pp. 209–10, e.g. 'if there be no real causation other than God's, every evil must be His direct act' (p. 210).

13. Tennant, *Philosophical Theology*, II, pp. 212, 122–9, 211.

14. Ibid., p. 212.

15. Flew, *God and Philosophy*, 4.29.

16. Farrer, *Finite and Infinite*, p. 22.

17. Flew, *God and Philosophy*, 4.44.

18. A. N. Whitehead, *Process and Reality: An Essay in Cosmology*, Gifford Lectures (New York: Harper & Row, 1960) p. 529.

19. A. N. Whitehead, *Modes of Thought* (Cambridge Univ. Press, 1938) p 207.

20. Flew, *God and Philosophy*, 4.18.

21. Owen, *Christian Knowledge of God*, p. 86.

22. A. Plantinga, *God and Other Minds* (Ithaca, N.Y.: Cornell Univ. Press, 1967) pp. 181–3.

23. P. Tillich, *Systematic Theology* (Welwyn: Nisbet, 1953) I, p. 182.

24. Martin, *Religious Belief*, p. 159 (to be interpreted in line with Tennant, cf. note 12 above).

25. Owen, *Christian Knowledge of God*, pp. 81–3.

26. Tennant, *Philosophical Theology*, II, chap. 7. Cf. Smart, *Philosophers and Religious Truth*, chap. 6.

27. Mascall, *Openness of Being*, p. 117.

28. Smart, *Philosophers and Religious Truth*, 4.22–3.

29. Flew, *God and Philosophy*, 4.45.

30. Munitz, *Mystery of Existence*, p. 125.

31. J. J. C. Smart, *Philosophy and Scientific Realism* (London: Routledge & Kegan Paul, 1963) pp. vii, 9–11.

32. Owen, *Christian Knowledge of God*, p. 87.

33. Whitehead, *Process and Reality*, p. 232; and a remark made by Whitehead in class as reported by P. A. Bertocci, *The Person God Is* (London: Allen & Unwin, 1971) p. 335 (cf. p. 225). These actual words are Bertocci's. Tennant speaks in similar vein of seeking to 'drive back the outposts of mystery to its irreducible stronghold, the ultimate' (*Philosophical Theology*, II, p. 211).

Chapter 5

1. See N. Smart, *The Yogi and the Devotee: The Interplay between the Upanishads and Catholic Theology* (London: Allen & Unwin, 1968) 2.70–86; 'Revelation, Reason and Religions', in I. T. Ramsey (ed.), *Prospect for Metaphysics* (London: Allen & Unwin, 1961); and *Philosophers and Religious Truth*, chap. 5. Cf. H. H. Farmer, *Revelation and Religion*, Gifford Lectures (Welwyn: Nisbet, 1954); Lewis, *Our Experience of God*, eg. pp. 65–99; and, most recently, J. Hick, *God and the Universe of Faiths* (London: Macmillan, 1973).

2. Smart, *Philosophers and Religious Truth*, 5.25.

3. Ibid., 5.52–3.

4. J. Jeremias, *The Central Message of the New Testament* (London: S.C.M. Press, 1965) pp. 16–17.

5. Ibid., pp. 19, 20.

6. Ibid., p. 21.

7. Ibid., pp. 25, 26–7.

8. Ibid., p. 30.

9. My support for the principle of natural explanation depends not only on the claims of unfettered inquiry, and on continued success in finding natural explanations for apparently inexplicable events, but also on the absence of (a sufficient number of sufficiently) well-attested occurrences which are *so* extraordinary that to deny that they are miracles – in the sense outlined for example by Swinburne – is downright preposterous or contrary to common sense. I would concede that such occurrences are indeed conceivable, and that if they occurred it might indeed be rational to regard them as violations of a law of nature and evidence of the intervening action of a god of some sort; but the extraordinary events which do in fact occur are not, it seems to me, of this kind. See R. G. Swinburne, *The Concept of Miracle* (London: Macmillan, 1970) *passim*, but esp. pp. 47–8, 58–9.

10. See B. Russell, *Religion and Science* (Oxford Univ. Press, 1935) pp. 26–7.

Chapter 6

1. T. Penelhum, 'Divine Necessity', *Mind*, LXIX (Apr 1960) 175–86.

2. E. E. Harris, *The Foundations of Metaphysics in Science* (London: Allen & Unwin, 1965).

3. Tennant, *Philosophical Theology*, II, p. 123.

4. Ibid.

5. See Plantinga, *God and Other Minds*, chap. 4. For a vigorous critique of the analogy between the cosmos and a product of design, which, however, tries to make too much capital out of the difficulty of laying down criteria for distinguishing products of design from undesigned entities, see W. I. Matson, *The Existence of God* (Ithaca, N.Y.: Cornell Univ. Press, 1965) pp. 122–31.

L. Pearl, 'Hume's Criticism of the Argument from Design', in *The Monist*, LIV (Apr 1970), argues that 'vegetation and generation, unlike design, do not provide explanations for the existence of orderly systems and processes but are, in fact, themselves illustrations of that very order which requires explanation'. 'There is no genesis of order here, but rather its transmission from one body to another' (p. 282). Yet it is impossible to say that generation is an illustration of that order which requires explanation without begging the question by assuming that the contrast between animals and products of human design is irrelevant. As an assumption, this is unfounded. (Alternatively, Pearl's remarks may be interpreted as leading to silly tenseless cosmic teleological questions of the kind rejected below.)

An appeal to the principle of parsimony in *support* of a teleological argument is made by R. G. Swinburne in his 'The Argument from Design', *Philosophy* (July 1968). He argues that explanation in terms of natural laws may ultimately be interpreted as explanation in terms of the action of a transcendent rational agent. Now some explanation is already in terms of the action of rational agents, and if the former interpretation is made, all explanation is reduced to personal explanation, a position which should be preferred by virtue of its greater simplicity. Swinburne has subsequently defended this view against criticisms made by A. Olding; cf. the latter's 'The Argument from Design – a Reply to R. G. Swinburne', *Religious Studies*, VII (Dec 1971) 361–73; R. G. Swinburne, 'The Argument from Design – a Defence', *Religious Studies*, VII (Sep 1972) 193–205. I would argue, however, that the putative gain in simplicity is offset both by having to posit this tremendous new entity, God, and by the fact that the interpretation of scientific theoretical explanation as personal explanation would be *in addition to* its apparently non-personal character as it stands, or involves also reducing scientific causal explanation to transcendent personal explanation, thereby abolishing the delegated autonomy of the world necessary for solving the problem of evil.

6. Tennant, *Philosophical Theology*, II, p. 79; Whitehead, *Process and Reality*, p. 508; cf. F. S. C. Northrop, 'The Macroscopic Atomic Theory: A Physical Interpretation of the Theory of Relativity', *Journal of Philosophy*, xxv (Aug 1928) 449–67.

7. Tennant, ibid., pp. 113, 82.

8. Smart, *Philosophers and Religious Truth*, 4.51, 4.53, 4.47–8.

9. Plantinga, *God and Other Minds*, p. 101.

10. Tennant, *Philosophical Theology*, II, p. 87.

11. Ibid., I, p. 283; II, p. 88; I, p. 289.

12. Ibid., II, pp. 88–9.

13. Hick, *Arguments for the Existence of God*, pp. 36, 34, 35.

14. See J. Richmond, *Theology and Metaphysics* (London: S.C.M. Press, 1970); B. Mitchell, *The Justificatiion of Religious Belief* (London: Macmillan, 1973). The former contains an excellent account of the relevant aspect of Wisdom's work; the latter might just allow Wisdom to be interpreted in such a way that the present study, with its accent on inference, may be regarded as exemplifying his approach; cf. the references to Wisdom in Chapter 10 below.

15. See I. T. Ramsey, *Models and Mystery* (London: Oxford Univ. Press, 1964) pp. 38–40; *Religion and Science*, pp. 65–75.

16. A. MacIntyre, *Difficulties in Christian Belief* (London: S.C.M. Press, 1959) p. 63. Cf. Flew's ten leaky buckets, *God and Philosophy*, 3.9.

Chapter 7

1. H. P. Owen, *Concepts of Deity* (London: Macmillan, 1970) pp. 19–20, 21.

2. Ibid., p. 20.

3. Mascall, *Openness of Being*, p. 168.

4. H. Meynell, *God and the World: The Coherence of Christian Theism* (London: S.P.C.K., 1971) p. 63.

5. J. N. Findlay, 'Can God's Existence be Disproved?', in Flew and MacIntyre (eds.), *New Essays in Philosophical Theology*, p. 51.

6. P. C. Appleby, 'On Religious Attitudes', *Religious Studies*, VI (Dec 1970) 368.

7. C. Hartshorne, *The Divine Relativity: A Social Conception of God* (New Haven: Yale Univ. Press, 1948) p. 38.

8. N. Pike, *God and Timelessness* (London: Routledge & Kegan Paul, 1970) pp. 189–90.

9. Hartshorne, *Divine Relativity*, pp. 45, 46, 48; Whitehead, *Process and Reality*, p. 528, italics added. The view contrary to Hartshorne's, that 'optimal dependence is zero dependence', receives rough treatment from him, being excoriated as 'this unwarranted assumption, this metaphysical snobbery toward relativity, dependence, or passivity, toward responsiveness or sensitivity, this almost slavish (doubtless it would be too much to say knavish) worship of mere absoluteness, independence, and one-sided activity or power, this transcendentalised admiration of politico-ecclesiastical tyranny, the ideal of which is to act on all while avoiding reaction from them, this spiritual blindness and false report upon experience' (ibid., p. 50).

10. Hartshorne, ibid., pp. 74, 90.

11. C. Hartshorne and W. L. Reese, *Philosophers Speak of God* (Univ. of Chicago Press, Phoenix Books, 1963) pp. 14–15. The distinction goes back to that between God's 'primordial nature' and his 'consequent nature' in Whitehead.

12. Hartshorne, *Divine Relativity*, p. 90.

13. Cf. Tennant, *Philosophical Theology*, II, pp. 140–3 (also p. 122).

14. J. Royce, *The Sources of Religious Insight* (Edinburgh: T. & T. Clark, 1912) p. 29.

15. N. Smart, 'Myth and Transcendence', *The Monist*, L (Oct 1966) 487. This is nevertheless a minor criticism of an excellent paper. Cf. J. A. T. Robinson, *Exploration into God* (London: S.C.M. Press, 1967) p. 38, n.1: 'Ultimately, of course, all spatial terms in relation to God are interchangeable.'

Chapter 8

1. J. Shepherd, 'Referring to God', *Religious Studies*, x (Mar 1974) 67–80.
2. N. Smart, *The Philosophy of Religion* (New York: Random House, 1970) p. 66.
3. Owen, *Christian Knowledge of God*, p. 211.
4. Ibid., pp. 214, 219.
5. Mascall, *Existence and Analogy*, p. 112.
6. See I. T. Ramsey, *Religious Language* (London: S.C.M. Press, 1957) chap. 2.
7. I. T. Ramsey, 'On Understanding Mystery', in J. H. Gill (ed.), *Philosophy and Religion* (Minneapolis: Burgess, 1968) p. 301.
8. I. T. Ramsey, *Christian Discourse: Some Logical Explorations* (London: Oxford Univ. Press, 1965) p. 89; *Models and Mystery*, pp. 38–40, 58; 'On the Possibility and Purpose of a Metaphysical Theology', in *Prospect for Metaphysics*, p. 172.
9. I. T. Ramsey, 'A Personal God', in F. G. Healey (ed.), *Prospect for Theology* (Welwyn: Nisbet, 1966) p. 70, italics added.
10. H. P. Owen, 'The Philosophical Theology of I. T. Ramsey', *Theology* (1970) 126; cf. Ramsey, 'A Personal God', p. 69.

Chapter 9

1. W. A. Christian, *Meaning and Truth in Religion* (Princeton Univ. Press, 1964).
2. Ibid., pp. 261–2.
3. Ibid., p. 49.
4. Ibid., p. 75.
5. F. Ferré, *Basic Modern Philosophy of Religion* (New York: Scribners, 1967) pp. 109–10, 357–61.
6. Christian, *Meaning and Truth in Religion*, p. 31.
7. Whitehead, *Process and Reality*, p. 37.
8. C. S. Peirce, 5.189, as quoted in K. T. Fann, *Peirce's Theory of Abduction* (The Hague: Nijhoff, 1971) p. 8. The numbers refer to C. Hartshorne and P. Weiss (eds.), *The Collected Papers of Charles Sanders Peirce* (Cambridge, Mass.: Harvard Univ. Press, 1931–5). The figures refer to the volume and to the numbered paragraphs in that volume.
9. See Fann, ibid., p. 9 and *passim*.
10. Peirce, 2.511, n.1, as quoted in Fann, ibid., pp. 8–9; 2.628, as quoted in Fann, ibid., p.21; 2.786, as quoted in T. A. Goudge, *The Thought of C. S. Peirce* (New York: Dover, 1969) p. 200.
11. Fann, ibid., p. 44.
12. See N. R. Hanson, *Patterns of Discovery* (Cambridge Univ. Press, 1958) chap. 4, esp. pp. 70–2, 84–90; and M. Polanyi, *Personal Knowledge*, Gifford Lectures (London: Routledge & Kegan Paul, 1962) chap. 1, esp. pp. 12–17.

13. The example is taken from P. Achinstein, *Law and Explanation* (Oxford: Clarendon Press, 1971) p. 101. Cf. ibid., pp. 104, 118.

14. See P. Geach, *God and the Soul* (London: Routledge & Kegan Paul, 1969) pp. 77–85.

15. Tillich, *Systematic Theology*, I, p. 11; K. Nielsen, *Contemporary Critiques of Religion* (London: Macmillan, 1971) p. 19.

16. Pontifex, *The Existence of God*, p. 147.

17. A. J. Ayer, *The Central Questions of Philosophy*, Gifford Lectures (London: Weidenfeld & Nicholson, 1973) pp. 134–5, 108,66, 33.

18. J. F. Ross, *Introduction to the Philosophy of Religion* (Toronto: Macmillan, 1969) p. 63.

19. Ibid., pp. 51–3.

20. Other and incisive criticisms of Ross, directed at his *Philosophical Theology*, are advanced by Hick in his *Arguments for the Existence of God*.

21. J. B. Cobb, Jr, *Living Options in Protestant Theology: A Survey of Methods* (Philadelphia: Westminster Press, 1962) pp. 312–18; *A Christian Natural Theology* (London: Lutterworth Press, 1965) pp. 252–70, esp. pp. 259–68.

22. By 'Winch–Phillips position' I mean Wittgensteinian fideism. See, e.g., P. Winch, 'Understanding a Primitive Society', in D. Z. Phillips (ed.), *Religion and Understanding* (Oxford: Blackwell, 1967) and in B. Wilson (ed.), *Rationality*. Other essays in both volumes are relevant. See too D. Z. Phillips, *The Concept of Prayer* (London: Routledge & Kegan Paul, 1965), and *Faith and Philosophical Enquiry* (London: Routledge & Kegan Paul, 1970); K. Nielsen, 'Wittgensteinian Fideism', *Philosophy*, XLII (July 1967) 191–209; and see note 4, Chapter 1 above.

23. Richmond, *Theology and Metaphysics*, I. 2.

24. Ibid., v.3, v.7, v.20.

25. J. Hick, *Faith and Knowledge*, 2nd ed. (London: Macmillan, 1967) p. 155; *Arguments for the Existence of God*, p. 33.

26. T. Penelhum, *Problems of Religious Knowledge* (London: Macmillan, 1971).

27. Ibid., pp. 62–3.

28. Christian, *Meaning and Truth in Religion*, pp. 165–6.

29. See F. C. S. Schiller, *Problems of Belief* (London: Hodder & Stoughton, 1918).

Chapter 10

1. T. Langan, 'Commentary' on Fr N. Clarke's paper in E. H. Madden, R. Handy and M. Farber (eds.), *The Idea of God: Philosophical Perspectives* (Springfield, Ill.: Charles Thomas, 1968) p. 36.

2. J. B. Mozley, *University Sermons*, 6th ed., p. 123, as quoted in Tennant, *Philosophical Theology*, II, p. 92. All other quotations are from Tennant, ibid., pp. 91–2.

3. Tennant, ibid., p. 92.

4. K. Walker, *Meaning and Purpose* (London: Jonathan Cape, 1944) p. 98.

5. Tennant, ibid., p. 93.

6. J. Jeans, *The Mysterious Universe* (Cambridge Univ. Press, 1930) p. 3.

7. For an illuminating discussion in these terms of the issues involved see A.

Flew and R. W. Hepburn, 'Problems of Perspective', *Plain View*, VII (1955) 151–66; cf. R. W. Hepburn, 'Questions about the Meaning of Life', *Religious Studies*, I (Apr 1966) 125–40.

8. J. Wisdom, 'Gods', in his *Philosophy and Psycho-Analysis* (Oxford: Blackwell, 1957) pp. 159–63; cf. Richmond, *Theology and Metaphysics*, III. 14–15.

9. Wisdom, ibid., p. 157.

10. F. Waismann, 'How I See Philosophy', in H. D. Lewis (ed.), *Contemporary British Philosophy*, Third Series (London: Allen & Unwin, 1924) pp. 480–1.

11. Mitchell, *Justification of Religious Belief*, p. 95, italics added. Cf. A. Jeffner, *The Study of Religious Language* (London: S.C.M. Press, 1972) pp. 120–31. Jeffner introduces the non-natural explanatory nature of putative religious statements as a solution to the problem of factual intelligibility. His discussion of current analyses of religious language is very useful, but, as he admits, he finally faces the inquirer with an ultimate choice between a merely scientific outlook and an explanatory metaphysical outlook, without any rational procedure for making the choice. This is because he does not make the explanatory metaphysical outlook dependent on the existence of genuine problems calling for non-natural explanation as opposed to mere transcendence-suggesting mysteries. Thus in this respect he does not advance beyond Hick's position. It may be that this is also true of Mitchell.

12. J. Butler, *The Analogy of Religion*, Introduction, sec. 4 (numerous editions).

13. W. James, 'The Will to Believe', in *The Will to Believe and Other Essays in Popular Philosophy* (New York: Longmans, Green & Co., 1897) p. 11 (and cf. his defence of Pascal, p. 6); ibid., pp. 3–4; Hick, *Faith and Knowledge*, p. 42.

14. Owen, *Christian Knowledge of God*, p. 157.

Bibliography

The following short selection of relevant literature is in addition
to the literature referred to in the notes:

Borst, C. V. (ed.), *The Mind–Brain Identity Theory* (London:
Macmillan, 1970; New York: St. Martin's Press, 1970).

Britton, Karl, *Philosophy and the Meaning of Life* (Cambridge and
New York: Cambridge Univ. Press, 1969).

Castell, Alburey, *The Self in Philosophy* (New York: Macmillan,
1965).

Clarke, W. Norris, S. J., 'A Curious Blindspot in the Anglo-
American Tradition of Antitheistic Argument', *The Monist*,
LIV (Apr 1970) 181–200.

Edwards, Paul, 'Why', article in Paul Edwards (ed.), *The Encyclopaedia of Philosophy* (New York: Macmillan, 1967).

Evans, Donald D., 'Ian Ramsey on Talk about God', *Religious
Studies*, VII (June 1971) 125–40; ibid., VII (Sept 1971) 213–26.

Flew, Antony, 'Tolstoy and the Meaning of Life', *Ethics*, LXXIII
(1963) 110–18.

Franklin, R. L., 'Necessary Being', *Australasian Journal of Philosophy*, XXXV (1957) 97–100.

Hartshorne, Charles, *A Natural Theology for Our Time* (La Salle,
Ill.: Open Court, 1967).

Hepburn, R. W., 'From World to God', *Mind*, LXXII (1963)
40–50; reprinted in Basil Mitchell (ed.), *The Philosophy of Religion* (London and Fair Laun, N. J. : Oxford Univ. Press.,
1971).

Hick, John H., 'God as Necessary Being', *Journal of Philosophy*,
LVII (1960) 725–34.

—— and McGill, A. C. (eds.), *The Many-Faced Argument: Recent
Studies on the Ontological Argument for the Existence of God*

(London and New York: Macmillan, 1968).

Hudson, W. D., *Ludwig Wittgenstein: The Bearing of his Philosophy upon Religious Belief* (London: Lutterworth, 1968; Richmond, Va.: John Knox Press, 1968).

Hutchings, P. A. E., 'Necessary Being', *Australasian Journal of Philosophy*, xxxv (1957) 201–6.

Knox, John, *Limits of Unbelief* (London: Collins, 1970).

Knox, John, Jr, 'Can the Self Survive the Death of its Mind?', *Religious Studies*, v (Oct 1969) 85–97.

    'Reply to Professor Woodhouse', *Religious Studies*, vi (Sept 1970) 273–80.

McPherson, Thomas, *The Argument from Design* (London: Macmillan, 1972: New York: St. Martin's Press, 1972).

Miles, T. R., *Religion and the Scientific Outlook* (London: Allen & Unwin, 1959; New York: Fernhill, 1959).

Mitchell, Basil (ed.), *The Philosophy of Religion* (London and Fair Lawn, N. J. Oxford Univ. Press, 1971).

Nielsen, Kai, *Scepticism* (London: Macmillan, 1973; New York: St. Martin's Press, 1973).

    'The Intelligibility of God-Talk', *Religious Studies*, vi (Mar 1970) 1–21.

Owen, H. P., *The Moral Argument for Christian Theism* (London: Allen & Unwin, 1965; New York: Humanities Press, 1965).

Palmer, Humphrey, *Analogy* (London: Macmillan, 1973; New York: St. Martin's Press, 1973).

Perrin, Norman, *Rediscovering the Teaching of Jesus* (London: S.C.M. Press, 1967; New York: Harper & Row, 1967).

Plantinga, Alvin, 'Necessary Being', in A. Plantinga (ed.), *Faith and Philosophy* (Grand Rapids, Mich.: Eerdman, 1964).

    (ed.), *The Ontological Argument from St Anselm to Contemporary Philosophers* (London: Macmillan, 1968; New York: Doubleday, 1965).

Ramsey, Ian T., 'The Systematic Elusiveness of "I"', *Philosophical Quarterly*, xxviii (1955)

    (ed.), *Biology and Personality: Frontier Problems in Science, Philosophy and Religion* (Oxford: Blackwell, 1965).

    (ed.), *Christian Ethics and Contemporary Philosophy* (London: S.C.M. Press, 1966; New York: Macmillan, 1966).

Reichenbach, Bruce R., 'Divine Necessity and the Cosmological Argument', *The Monist*, liv (July 1970) 401–15.

Ross, James F., 'On Proofs for the Existence of God', *The Monist*, LIV (Apr 1970) 201–17.

Rowe, William L., 'Two Criticisms of the Cosmological Argument', *The Monist*, LIV (July 1970) 441–59.

Smart, Ninian, 'Mystical Experience', *Sophia*, I (Apr 1962) 19–26.

  'Interpretation and Mystical Experience', *Religious Studies*, I (Oct 1965) 75–87.

Tennant, F. R., *The Nature of Belief* (London: Centenary Press, 1943).

Trethowan, Dom Illtyd, *Absolute Value: A Study in Christian Theism* (London: Allen & Unwin, 1970; New York: Humanities Press, 1970).

  'Flew's "God and Philosophy" ', *Downside Review*, LXXXVIII (Jan 1970) 1–13.

Wittgenstein, Ludwig, *Lectures and Conversations on Aesthetics, Psychology, and Religious Belief*, ed. Cyril Barrett (Oxford: Blackwell, 1966; Berkeley: Univ. of California Press, 1967).

Woodhouse, Mark B., 'Selves and Minds: A Reply to Professor Knox', *Religious Studies*, VI (Sept 1970) 263–72.

Index